13

VERY BAD
DAYS

and How God Fixed Them

13
VERY BAD
DAYS
and How God Fixed Them

DAVID **C** COOK

transforming lives together

13 VERY BAD DAYS AND HOW GOD FIXED THEM
Published by David C Cook
4050 Lee Vance Drive
Colorado Springs, CO 80918 U.S.A.

Integrity Music Limited, a Division of David C Cook
Eastbourne, East Sussex BN23 6NT, England

The graphic circle C logo is a registered trademark of David C Cook.

LCCN 2017952543
ISBN 978-0-7847-2122-3
eISBN 978-0-8307-7299-5

© 2018 David C Cook
Developed by Standard Publishing.

The Team: Lindsay Black, Amy Konyndyk, Rachael
Stevenson, Abby DeBenedittis, Susan Murdock
Cover Design/Illustration: Dennis Jones

Printed in the United States of America

2 3 4 5 6 7 8 9 10 11

103118

"This is the day the L<small>ORD</small> has made.
We will rejoice and be glad in it."

Psalm 118:24

Contents

How to Use These
Sessions

About These Sessions

First, thanks. Thanks for caring about children and for helping them see that even a "bad day" holds amazing surprises. That's what the people who experienced the "bad days" described in these 13 sessions discovered—and what your kids will discover too.

With God, bad days are a chance for God to show his power!

Welcome to Easy

These sessions for elementary kids are carefully designed to make your life easy. They're light on supplies, quick to prepare, and long on fun. You'll find most supplies in the church's supply closet or kitchen or at home in your garage, pantry, or junk drawer—no need to spend time ordering materials online.

Because these sessions are created so beginning teachers or mature teenagers can lead them confidently, you won't need highly trained teachers. And the variety of options in each session will snag the attention—and hold it—of first-grade through sixth-grade children, including the boys!

Best of all, you'll see kids grow in their faith as they open their hearts to what God shares with them through these 13 sessions.

Welcome to Simple Learning

Preparation is easy too. Each week you'll focus on one key Bible truth, which children will explore and apply. You'll drive that point home through

Bible exploration, fun discussion, giggle-worthy games, and "Oh, wow!" activities that engage kids in multiple ways through multiple learning styles.

Welcome to Deep Bible Discovery

Each week, your children will actually *experience* a Bible story. They'll discover it, ponder it, talk about it, pray about it, and apply what they learn. If that's what you're looking for—for your children to *do* God's Word instead of just hear it—you're in exactly the right place. And here's a tip: supersize the learning by using a kid-friendly version of the Bible to make sure the stories are understood by children.

Welcome to Flexibility

We get it: sometimes you have to punt. A sermon goes long ... or short. Kids are quick to dive into a lesson or need some time to warm up to being together. Older kids might zip through an activity while their younger friends take longer.

Relax. We've got you covered.

You can use these sessions with kids in practically any setting: in Sunday school, children's church, evening programs, or while kids' parents are attending an adult class or small group. There's maximum flexibility because each session is written to last 45 minutes and then provides enough extras to fill a full hour. These sessions stretch to fit exactly what you need, when you need it. They're ...

- **multi-aged**—suitable for mixed ages of elementary children;
- **easily adapted**—sessions work for just a couple kids or a packed classroom;
- **relational**—children grow close to Jesus *and* one another;
- **flexible**—brimming with options to fit varying time frames; and
- **fun**—even easily distracted kids can engage, learn, and grow.

So are you ready for some fun? Let's dive in!

Noah's

Bad Day

The Point: God wants us to obey him.

Scripture Connect: Genesis 6:5–7:5

Supplies for all Session 1 activities options: pencils, prepared poster, 10 index cards per child, Bibles, paper

The Basics for Leaders

When God interrupted Noah's life with instructions to build an ark, Noah wasn't looking for new projects. He was already busy raising a family. He had flocks and herds to tend. He was living his life.

But in a single day Noah received two challenging pieces of news. First, he was supposed to drop everything and gather materials, round up animals, and hammer together a floating zoo. And second, there was a flood coming. A big flood. Suddenly, what seemed like a strange request made perfect sense. Noah needed to build an ark—and the sooner he got started, the better.

God asks us to do things that don't make sense too. At least, they don't make sense at first glance …

Turn the other cheek when someone hurts us?

Forgive our enemies?

Give away a chunk of our income from every paycheck or allowance?

Silly. Senseless. Pointless. Except … God knows something is coming that requires we value what he values, that we obey God and let him shape our hearts and minds. If we're followers of Jesus, we'll be with God for eternity. We're learning how to obey God for when we get to our real home—heaven. Noah obeyed God, and as raindrops splashed against the ark's deck, he was reminded yet again that God always wants us to obey him—and that's a wise choice!

OPENING ACTIVITY—OPTION 1

HOWZITGOIN'

Time: about 5 minutes, depending on attendance
Supplies: pencils, prepared poster

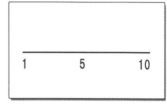

Before kids arrive, draw a line on a poster. Write a 1 on the left end of the line, a 10 on the right, and a 5 in the middle. As kids arrive, ask them to pencil in their initials on the line.

Say: **If this past week was so awful you wish you'd slept through it, place your initials by the 1. If it was a great week you wish you could repeat, put your initials by the 10. Place your initials anywhere on the line that shows how you feel about this past week—except exactly on the 5. Because there's no such thing as a week that's exactly half good and half bad!**

After kids have signed in, give them 30 seconds each to explain why they placed their initials where they did. Be sure to include your own initials and explain your placement on the line. Kids will begin to express themselves more over time, and hearing their stories will help you adapt this lesson to make it relevant to your kids' lives.

OPENING ACTIVITY—OPTION 2

SOAP OR A ROPE?

Time: about 10 minutes
Supplies: none

Ask children to stand in a single line, facing you. Tell them you're going to ask them to make a choice between pairs of imaginary items. If they choose the first item you mention, they're to take a step to the right. If they choose the second item, they'll take a step to the left. One rule: they *must* make a choice. They can't stay on the line. (If you have young kids who may not know their right and left directions, consider taping sheets of paper to the walls on either side of the room; one with an L for left and the other with an R for right. Or have kids step forward and backward instead of left and right.)

Read each pair of choices below. Then pause. After each forced choice, read the second part of the option. Six are provided to get you started—feel free to add your own!

- Would you rather have soap or a rope ... to wash yourself in the shower?
- Would you rather have shampoo or milk ... to put on breakfast cereal?
- Would you rather have soda pop or water ... to keep your plants healthy?
- Would you rather have your head or your feet ... stuffed inside a shoe?
- Would you rather have lots of Chihuahuas or Great Danes ... to juggle?
- Would you rather have toilet tissue or printer paper ... to write on?

Ask children to find partners and discuss the following questions. (If you have five or fewer children in attendance, simply get in a circle and have the discussion as a group.)

- How did you make your choices?
- Why was it hard to always make the choice that made sense?

Affirm kids' answers and their involvement. Then say: **It was hard to pick the item that made sense before you knew how it would be used. That's probably how it was with Noah. It didn't make sense to the people around him that Noah was building a huge ark. But Noah knew something others didn't know: God was sending a flood!**

Some things God asks us to do, such as forgiving others, giving away some of the money we receive, or loving people who aren't nice to us, may not make sense either—except we know God is helping shape us to be like him, to care about what he cares about. God wants us to obey him. It's important we obey God because he's getting us ready to live with him in heaven. Obeying God is always a wise choice!

Bad Days Game

BUILD IT!

Time: 10 minutes or more, as desired
Supplies: 10 index cards (you're willing to lose) for each child

Ask children to form groups of three. Give each group 30 index cards.

Say: **Time to build a card tower for me. I want you to make one that's as high as possible. Pick a spot on the floor to start construction and take four minutes to see what you can do. Start now!** (If you have young children, demonstrate how to place cards to build a card house. Consider pairing each young child with two older kids.)

Give a one-minute and 30-second warning. Adding the time pressure makes a tough challenge even more challenging for older kids! (Note: most of your groups won't be able to even begin building a tower—but their frustration will help make their later accomplishment sweeter!)

After four minutes, have children show what they were able to accomplish. Then say: **I'm going to give you the same assignment, but this time I'm going to be like God giving instructions to Noah when Noah was to build an ark. I'll give you detailed instructions.**

This time, you can bend the cards like this. Demonstrate bending a card to make a right angle. **This lets you build walls that are more stable. See how high you can go this time. Ready? Go!**

You'll see a dramatic difference in the height of the towers! Once again, give one-minute and 30-second warnings, and again let kids show off their work. Say: **It helps when we get good instructions, doesn't it? Let's take a look at what God told Noah when it came to boat building. But before we start, we'll pick up the cards.**

Collect cards to straighten and reuse or to recycle.

Bad Days Bible Story

SIGNS, SIGNS, EVERYWHERE A SIGN

Time: about 15 minutes
Supplies: Bible(s), 1 sheet of paper and pencil per child

Say: **Let's pretend you see a fence surrounding a house, a fence 10 feet high with barbed wire on top. A sign is nailed to the fence: "Stay Out!**

Beware Killer Dogs." Behind the fence you hear snarling and snapping teeth. Would you obey the sign? Why or why not?

As children discuss, pass out a pencil and sheet of paper to each person. (If you have young children who cannot write well yet, pair them with older kids.)

Say: **Obeying signs about killer dogs might save your life! On your paper, draw another sign that might save a life—if people obey it. Your sign can be real, like "Slow Down—Dangerous Curve Ahead." Or make something up, like "Don't Walk Under Sofa—Monster Dust Bunny Zone."**

Provide encouragement. After a few minutes, ask kids to show their signs to the larger group. Then say: **Obeying signs can be important. Obeying God is always important, just as Noah found out. As I read this brief account about Noah aloud, listen for two things:**

AGE-ALERT TIPS

If you have mostly **older children** (4th, 5th, and 6th graders), modify the lesson in these ways:

Alert #1: Add another debriefing question: Why do you, at times, find it challenging to obey God?

Alert #2: Provide enough Bibles so pairs can read the Scripture passage independently.

- **In what ways was Noah obedient to God?**
- **How was obeying God a good thing for Noah? A challenge?**

Read aloud Genesis 6:5–7:5. Even better: ask competent, confident readers in your group to take turns reading aloud. (If your group is younger or you wish to read a shorter passage, read aloud Gen. 6:9–22.)

After hearing the passage, ask children to form pairs to discuss the questions. Not many kids? Stay in one group for the discussion. Read the questions above aloud again.

If children are talking in pairs, invite them to report back to the group. Then ask kids to turn over their sheets of paper and pick up their pencils.

Say: **Noah's not the only one who's supposed to obey God. That's our job too.**

Read aloud John 14:23–24.

On the backs of the signs, ask children to create new signs that remind them to obey God in specific areas. For instance, a child's sign might read,

"Do What Your Mother Says—the FIRST Time She Asks." That's a reminder to honor parents in a specific way. Kids can choose to use words or pictures to make their signs. Give kids up to four minutes to create their signs.

When the signs are finished, say: **We all need reminders to obey God at home, at school, even here. Let's show our signs and see if any of us share the same challenges.**

After reviewing the signs, tell children to take their signs home to post in a spot they'll see daily as reminders to always obey God. But before putting away the signs, ask children to sit in a circle and hold their signs. Move into the Sign Prayer.

CLOSING PRAYER

SIGN PRAYER

Time: about 3 minutes
Supplies: signs kids drew in the previous activity

Say: **God was serious: we need to obey him. When we don't obey we're sinning—not doing what God wants. Please hold your signs as I lead us in prayer.**

Dear God, we all hold signs that are reminders of how we sometimes find it hard to obey you. We know that obeying you honors you. Obeying you is good for us. But still it can be hard for us.

Please forgive us for not obeying you.

Please give us hearts that want to please you. And please help us do what Noah did: obey you no matter what!

In Jesus's name, amen.

Ask kids to fold their signs and tuck them in their pockets or set them aside to take home.

EXTRA-TIME ACTIVITY—OPTION 1

TWO-BY-TWO

Time: about 5 minutes
Supplies: none

The animals made it onto Noah's ark in pairs. See if your kids can quickly fill in the matching piece of each pair listed below. Call out the first portion of each pair and see what kids say. Suggestions are in parentheses, but there are no wrong answers! When you're finished with the list, invite kids to brainstorm their own word pairs.

- Milk and … (cookies)
- Salt and … (pepper)
- Shoes and … (socks)
- Up and … (down)
- Apples and … (oranges)

- Peanut butter and … (jelly)
- Cats and … (dogs)
- Ham and … (cheese)
- Bits and … (pieces)
- Odds and … (ends)

EXTRA-TIME ACTIVITY—OPTION 2

DO THE MATH
Time: about 5 minutes (or never, depending on your math abilities!)
Supplies: pencils, paper

Just how big *was* the ark? Direct children to Genesis 6:15–16 and ask them to figure out the square footage of the ark.

EXTRA-TIME ACTIVITY—OPTION 3

INQUIRING MINDS WANT TO KNOW
Time: 5 minutes
Supplies: none

Gather kids in a circle. Ask: **What is a rule at home or school you always obey and why? What might happen if you disobeyed? How does obeying keep us happy and safe?**

Joseph's Bad Day

The Point: God is in control.
Scripture Connect: Genesis 37:12–36

Supplies for all Session 2 activities options: pencils, prepared poster, Bible, 1 quarter for each child to keep, paper, popped popcorn, 1 clean bed-sheet or blanket

The Basics for Leaders

When Joseph hiked out to check on his brothers, he was a favored younger son—one wearing an expensive coat and a big grin. By nightfall, Joseph was almost naked and was a slave on his way to Egypt. Joseph had been betrayed by his own brothers. Now that's a bad day … or was it?

Fast-forward a few years and Joseph himself tells his brothers it was God who sent him to Egypt, and they didn't need to be angry with themselves for what they'd done in getting him there (Gen. 45:5).

Yes, it was a bad day when Joseph was dragged into slavery. And when his brothers stripped him and sold him like an unwanted donkey, Joseph felt the pain. But God did something amazing with Joseph's bad day just as he can do something amazing with ours.

Today you'll help your kids discover what Joseph discovered: in the end, God is in control.

OPENING ACTIVITY—OPTION 1

HOWZITGOIN'

Time: about 5 minutes, depending on attendance
Supplies: pencils, prepared poster

Before kids arrive, draw a line on a poster.
Write a 1 on the left end of the line, a 10 on
the right, and a 5 in the middle. As kids arrive,
ask them to pencil in their initials on the line.

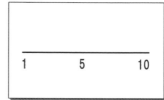

Say: **If this past week was so awful
you wish you'd slept through it, place your initials by the 1. If it was a
great week you wish you could repeat, put your initials by the 10. Place
your initials anywhere on the line that shows how you feel about this
past week—except exactly on the 5. Because there's no such thing as a
week that's exactly half good and half bad!**

After kids have signed in, give them 30 seconds each to explain why they
placed their initials where they did. Be sure to include your own initials and
explain your placement on the line. Kids will begin to express themselves
more over time, and hearing their stories will help you adapt this lesson to
make it relevant to your kids' lives.

OPENING ACTIVITY—OPTION 2

NOT SO FAST!

Time: about 10 minutes
Supplies: none

Ask children to pick partners.

Say: **I want you to find ways to make a situation worse. For example,
if I say, "We went to the beach and the water was warm" you might say,
"Not so fast! The shark that ate Lenny thought the water was warm too!"**

**No matter what I say, with your partner find a way to turn it into a
disaster. And always begin with "Not so fast!" Ready? Let's go!**

After reading each of the following statements, pause to let pairs respond.
Move quickly from one statement to the next. Add more statements of your
own if you wish.

- My new bicycle is right outside.
- Our teacher is really good—I'm learning a lot.
- My family's taking a trip to the mountains.
- Our team has won six games in a row.
- You're invited to my birthday party!

When finished, invite partners to give each other high fives. Then ask children to sit in a circle and discuss:

- If you could get a "do over" on any day in your life, what day would you pick—and why?

AGE-ALERT TIPS

If you have mostly **early elementary children**, substitute the following, easier situations:

- On my new bicycle, I can ride fast.
- My puppy likes to lick my face.
- I have an ice cream cone with five scoops stacked up.
- I hit a baseball at Mrs. Lillicut's house.

Say: **Sometimes tough days happen. What starts out positive and fun can sometimes end in disaster. We wish we could control those days, but we can't. In the Bible, Joseph discovered something we'll discover too: though we're not in control, God is. He's even in control when our days are dark and difficult.**

Joseph started a day by taking a walk in the sunshine, going off to see his brothers. By the end of the day, he'd been stripped of his fine clothes and sold into slavery. Joseph discovered that he didn't have control over the situation, but God did! Let's dig deeper to see what we can control and what we can't—and what God can control.

Bad Days Game

MONKEY FACE

Time: 5 minutes or more, as desired
Supplies: none

Say: **When you look in a mirror and make a face, the mirror makes a face right back at you—even if it's a funny face, like a monkey face.**

Ask children to find partners and stand facing their partners. Say: **Whoever has the darkest shoes will go first in this exercise. You'll move and your partner will mirror what you do. What you do is up to you. Make a monkey face like this.** (demonstrate) **Or jump.** (demonstrate) **What you do, your partner will do. You have 30 seconds. Go!**

After 30 seconds, have partners switch roles. Then have kids be seated and ask:

- **Which was most fun: leading or following? Why?**
- **Which was easier: leading or following? Why?**

After kids answer, say: **It's fun to be in charge when you get to call the shots. You know what's coming next. You get to do what you want. But are we ever really in control or in charge? Let's see what we can learn from Joseph about being in control!**

Bad Days Bible Story

JOSEPH CIRCLE

Time: about 15 minutes
Supplies: Bible

Ask children to go to the center of the room and stand in a circle, facing inward, and with about a foot between kids.

Say: **Let's find out what happened to a man named Joseph. He lived hundreds of years before Jesus was on the earth. Joseph had 10 older brothers, and they all hated him because Joseph was his father's favorite. Joseph was treated better than his brothers. Plus he tattled on**

AGE-ALERT TIPS

If you have mostly **older children** (4th, 5th, and 6th graders), modify the lesson in these ways:
Alert #1: Pass the Bible around so children can read the passages aloud.
Alert #2: Add this as a last debriefing question: *How might your life be different if you gave more control to God?*

his brothers. And in his dreams, which he shared with his brothers, he was always in charge of them. How would you feel about your brother or sister if all that happened?** (pause for responses)

I'll read what happened to Joseph. When you hear something you think made Joseph's day a good one, take a half step forward. If you hear

something you think made Joseph's day a bad one, take a step backward. We may not all agree what's good and bad, or move at the same time, but that's fine. We'll see where we end up.

Read aloud Genesis 37:12–14, 18–24, 28. Pause to let children see where they're standing. Say: **Looks like we think Joseph had a tough few days.**

As a group, still standing where you are, discuss:

- **How much control over what happened do you think Joseph had?**

Say: **Joseph's story doesn't end there. He was sold to an important man in Egypt, jailed for something he didn't do, noticed by Pharaoh, and freed. He even saw his brothers again.**

Read Genesis 39:1–4, 20–22; 41:41–43; 45:1, 5, 8. Have kids continue stepping forward or backward as you read. Then see where children are standing now.

Say: **Joseph may not have been in charge, but God was. God saved thousands of lives through Joseph in Egypt, something Joseph couldn't have done unless he'd been dragged to Egypt.**

Ask children to sit in a circle and discuss:

- **How much control do you think God had over what happened to Joseph?**
- **Why is it better for God to be in control than for us to be in control?**
- **What are things that God controls in our lives?**
- **What's one thing you could change that would give God more control in your life?**

CLOSING PRAYER

COIN-FLIP PRAYER

Time: about 10 minutes
Supplies: 1 quarter for each child to keep

Give each child a quarter. Ask children to try and flip their coins and catch them in the air. If some children don't know how to do this, ask older kids who have developed the skill to demonstrate.

After several flips, invite children to form pairs. Say: **Let's flip coins at the same time and see what comes up: heads or tails. If it's heads, tell your partner about a tough thing that happened this week. If it's tails, tell your partner about something fun that happened this week. If you tie, flip again!**

Give partners time to flip their coins several times and share. Then say: **Keep your fists closed so nobody can tell which hand you're using to hold your coin. If you feel you're having mostly tough days lately, hold the coin in you right hand. Everything seem easy this week? Place the coin in your left hand. Now close your eyes and pray with me.**

Dear God, you're in control of both our easy days and the tough ones. That's a hard truth for us. Please help us trust and know that you're in control even when things are difficult. Like Joseph, we want to serve you well on all of our days, whether they're hard or easy ones.

In Jesus's name, amen.

Tell kids to keep the quarters as reminders that God is in control even when our days might be tough or frustrating. Ask children to pray during the week whenever they take out the quarters from their pockets.

EXTRA-TIME ACTIVITY—OPTION 1

BRING IT IN FOR A LANDING

Time: about 10 minutes
Supplies: 1 sheet of paper per child

Give each child a sheet of paper and this challenge: in two minutes, craft a paper airplane to launch toward a wastebasket target on the other side of the room. The goal: bring your plane in for a landing inside the basket. (If you have younger kids, pair them with older kids who know how to fold paper airplanes.) Have kids explain their designs before launching their planes. Then, taking turns, send the creations off into the wild, blue yonder. See who comes closest to the target. Then discuss the following:

- **What helped the winning plane have more control than the others?**
- **What helps you have self-control in your life?**
- **Why is letting God have control of your life a good idea?**

EXTRA-TIME ACTIVITY—OPTION 2

POPCORN CATCH

Time: about 5 minutes
Supplies: popped popcorn, 1 clean bedsheet or blanket

You may want to cover the carpet with a clean bedsheet or blanket before trying this. Check with the person in charge of the place where you're meeting!

Give each child five kernels of popped popcorn. Demonstrate how to toss a piece in the air and catch it in your open mouth—or how to *almost* catch it there. Your kids will catch on!

Explain that the goal of this activity is to have enough eye-hand-mouth control to snag five out of five kernels. After kids have tried out their popcorn-catching skills, serve more popcorn and discuss the following questions:

- **What helps someone get better as a popcorn catcher?**
- **What helps us do a better job of letting God have control of our lives?**

EXTRA-TIME ACTIVITY—OPTION 3

INQUIRING MINDS WANT TO KNOW

Time: 5 minutes
Supplies: none

Gather kids in a circle. Ask: **If you were being dragged off to Egypt as a slave, how certain would you be that God was in control? Why?**

Moses's

Bad Day

The Point: God has a plan.
Scripture Connect: Exodus 14:5–31

Supplies for all Session 3 activities options: pencils, prepared poster, paper, safety scissors (several), 1 adult-size button-up shirt for every 2 kids, 3 Bibles, box of facial tissues or damp paper towels, saucers, tempera paint or water-based highlighters (not yellow), newspapers, 3 rolled-up socks per child

The Basics for Leaders

Moses had a good run going. Following God's instructions, he'd managed to pry hundreds of thousands of his people out of Pharaoh's grasp. They'd left Egypt, found a way to get organized, and stayed together on the long march.

But now here Moses was: the Red Sea in front of him, an Egyptian army behind him, and the people in a panic. What should they do, the people wanted to know. What was the plan?

Here's the truth: Moses didn't have a plan, but God did. A plan for that day, the next day, all the way to the Promised Land. Moses discovered again he could trust God, that faithfully following God's plan was what God required of Moses. And while Moses might not know what to do next, God had a plan for Moses—and God has a plan for us too!

OPENING ACTIVITY—OPTION 1

HOWZITGOIN'

Time: about 5 minutes, depending on attendance
Supplies: pencils, prepared poster

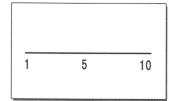

Before kids arrive, draw a line on a poster. Write a 1 on the left end of the line, a 10 on the right, and a 5 in the middle. As kids arrive, ask them to pencil in their initials on the line.

Say: **If this past week was so awful you wish you'd slept through it, place your initials by the 1. If it was a great week you wish you could repeat, put your initials by the 10. Place your initials anywhere on the line that shows how you feel about this past week—except exactly on the 5. Because there's no such thing as a week that's exactly half good and half bad!**

After kids have signed in, give them 30 seconds each to explain why they placed their initials where they did. Be sure to include your own initials and explain your placement on the line. Kids will begin to express themselves more over time, and hearing their stories will help you adapt this lesson to make it relevant to your kids' lives.

OPENING ACTIVITY—OPTION 2

ACCORDING TO PLAN

Time: about 10 minutes
Supplies: paper, safety scissors (several)

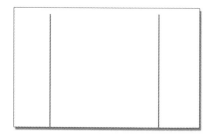

Give each child a sheet of paper and a pair of safety scissors.

Show children how to turn the paper sideways (landscape position) and make two cuts that go almost to the top of the paper (see diagram). If you don't have enough safety scissors for each child to have a pair, let children take turns. (Invite older kids to help younger ones do the cutting if needed.)

Say: **Hold your papers on the sides. When I say "go," pull on both sides, ripping the paper so the middle section falls straight down. Ready? Go!**

As children tear the papers, they'll notice that the center sections don't flutter straight to the floor. Give children a chance to try again with new sheets of paper, if desired.

Say: **Good plan, but it didn't work. Why do you think that's true?**

Take suggestions. If they aren't mentioned, add these reasons: it's hard to pull both sides precisely the same and the cuts probably aren't identical.

Say: **We often come up with great plans that don't work out. Find a partner and describe a plan of yours that sounded great, but failed. Or share another plan you know of that didn't work out.**

Allow time for partners to share. Then say: **Today we'll explore what Moses discovered about God's plans.**

Bad Days Game

BUTTON IT UP

Time: about 10 minutes
Supplies: 1 adult-size button-up shirt for every 2 kids

Invite children to find partners. Ask the child in each pair whose birthday is closest to Christmas to close his or her eyes. Hand the other child in each pair an unbuttoned shirt.

Have the children with their eyes closed describe to their partners how to put on the shirt and button it. Here's the catch: the person with eyes open in each pair must do exactly what's said—and *only* what's said.

After two minutes, have children giving instructions open their eyes and see how their instructions worked out. Then have partners switch roles and repeat the activity.

Retrieve the shirts and say: **Sometimes our directions don't always make sense—even if we plan to do something simple like buttoning up a shirt. But God's directions and plans are perfect, even if we don't always understand why he's asking us to do something.**

Bad Days Bible Story

MOSES JIGSAW

Time: about 20 minutes
Supplies: 3 Bibles

Form your children into three groups. Give each group a Bible and help groups find Exodus 14. (A group could be one child, and if necessary, you can be a group.) If you have non-readers or younger kids, pair them with older kids who can read to them.

Explain that you'll give each group a passage to read and act out in private. Tell kids they will have a chance to act out their passages for the whole group in a few minutes. Assign one of the following passages to each group. Allow several minutes for groups to read and prepare, checking in to see that everyone understands what he or she is reading.

Group 1: Exodus 14:5–14
Group 2: Exodus 14:15–22
Group 3: Exodus 14:23–31

After groups present their portions of Moses' story in order, discuss the following as a larger group:

AGE-ALERT TIPS

If you have mostly **early elementary children**, the reading may be too challenging, but the acting will be fun! Either read the passage aloud as children instantly act out what they hear, or assign a capable reader in each small group so younger children can listen and then plan how to act out the story.

- **Was it fair that God didn't share his whole plan with Moses? Why or why not?**
- **Does it seem fair that God hasn't told you what he has planned for all of your life? Why or why not?**

Say: **God doesn't give us all the details about what will happen to us. But God has a plan for everything and everyone—and he knows you and will be with you forever.**

Close the activity by reading aloud Matthew 10:29–31 and John 11:25–26. Remind kids that God has a plan for us all.

CLOSING PRAYER

POPCORN PRAYER

Time: about 3 minutes
Supplies: none

Have children sit on the floor in a circle.

Say: **Let's offer God one-word prayers today. Think of a word that says how you feel about knowing God has a plan for your life. Maybe that word is** *comforting* **because you feel loved knowing God cares for you and your future. Maybe that word is** *afraid* **because you think you won't be able to do what God has for you to do. Think of your own word now.**

I'll open our prayer. When you have a word in mind, pop up to your feet, say it out loud, and then sit again. I'll close for us.

Participate yourself by offering a word. Begin simply with, "Dear God, please hear our prayer" and end with a simple "In Jesus's name, amen."

EXTRA-TIME ACTIVITY—OPTION 1

FINGERPRINT

Time: about 10 minutes
Supplies: 1 sheet of paper and pencil per child, a box of facial tissues or damp paper towels, saucers, tempera paint or water-based highlighters (not yellow), newspapers

Cover a table with newspapers. Pour a bit of tempera paint in a saucer and place it on the newspaper. Give each child a sheet of paper. (If you don't have paints, simply use a colored, water-based highlighter to "paint" each child's thumb or finger pad and make a print on his or her sheet of paper.)

Invite kids to dip their thumb or finger pads into the paint and stamp the prints on the paper. Wipe off excess paint with a facial tissue or damp paper towels.

Have children compare their fingerprints or thumbprints, looking closely at the patterns of swirls. Remind children their fingerprints are unique; no two are quite the same.

Give children pencils and encourage them to draw a picture of themselves, somehow incorporating their fingerprints or thumbprints as an element in their photos. For example, the print could be a head or a tummy or even a flower beside their self-portraits.

After children show each other their self-portraits, say: **God's plans for us are like our fingerprints—all are the same in some ways, but all are a bit different. But one thing we're sure of: God does have a plan for us, and as we follow Jesus, we'll discover what it is!**

EXTRA-TIME ACTIVITY—OPTION 2

SOCK ROTATION

Time: about 5 minutes (or never, depending on your math abilities!)
Supplies: 3 rolled-up socks per child

Give each child at least three rolled-up socks. Explain that juggling is actually easy—you just plan how to throw several socks in the air in rotation so you can keep them up and moving. The plan is easy.

Challenge kids to plan how they will juggle the socks; then see how the plans go.

If you have a juggler in your group, ask for a group tutoring session. It will help your juggler feel special and send everyone home with a new skill.

After attempting juggling, have children circle up and discuss:

- **What does it take for a plan to work?**
- **What's a plan you have for your life?**
- **What do you think God has planned for you?**

EXTRA-TIME ACTIVITY—OPTION 3

INQUIRING MINDS WANT TO KNOW

Time: 5 minutes
Supplies: none

Gather kids in a circle. Ask: **Plan your perfect day. What would you do? Where would you go? Who would you be with? If God was planning a perfect day for you, what would it include?**

Daniel's

Bad Day

The Point: God wants us to trust him.
Scripture Connect: Daniel 6:1–24

Supplies for all Session 4 activities options: pencils, prepared poster, 20 paper cups (same size; not foam or plastic), 2 squares of sturdy cardboard (24" x 24"), Bible, jigsaw puzzle with box, newspapers, wastebasket, $5 bill for each child (not to keep)

The Basics for Leaders

It's easy to trust God when everything is going well. When, like Daniel, you have a good job, a nice place to live, friends, when people trust you and look up to you.

But what about when others seek to do you harm? Or when hungry lions circle around you, growling in the dark? How easy is it to trust God then?

Daniel got to find out how it felt in both of those situations. His comfy life became very uncomfortable when he was accused, and rightly so, of praying to God. And because Daniel's enemies planned ahead, they got him tossed into a cave where he was supposed to be torn apart by lions—except that's not quite what happened. The lions got lunch, all right, but it wasn't Daniel. What Daniel got was a memorable reminder that we can trust God just as he desires us to. You'll help children discover the same thing today!

OPENING ACTIVITY—OPTION 1

HOWZITGOIN'

Time: about 5 minutes, depending on attendance
Supplies: pencils, prepared poster

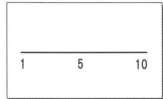

Before kids arrive, draw a line on a poster. Write a 1 on the left end of the line, a 10 on the right, and a 5 in the middle. As kids arrive, ask them to pencil in their initials on the line.

Say: **If this past week was so awful you wish you'd slept through it, place your initials by the 1. If it was a great week you wish you could repeat, put your initials by the 10. Place your initials anywhere on the line that shows how you feel about this past week—except exactly on the 5. Because there's no such thing as a week that's exactly half good and half bad!**

After kids have signed in, give them 30 seconds each to explain why they placed their initials where they did. Be sure to include your own initials and explain your placement on the line. Kids will begin to express themselves more over time, and hearing their stories will help you adapt this lesson to make it relevant to your kids' lives.

OPENING ACTIVITY—OPTION 2

STANDING ON THE PROMISES

Time: about 15 minutes
Supplies: 20 paper cups (same size; not foam or plastic), 2 squares of sturdy cardboard (24" X 24")

Place a cardboard square on a non-skid floor surface (such as on carpeting or a large rug).

Say: **Lots of people make promises and then say "trust me." But can you really trust that person? How can you tell if someone can be trusted?** Take suggestions. If it's not mentioned, add this: you test little promises before deciding to trust a big one.

Hand each child several cups. (You'll want to go through 20 cups in all.) Say: **What's a promise God has made to you? For each promise we can remember, we'll place a cup upside down on this cardboard.**

If you come up short of 20 promises, read the following passages aloud and ask children what promise they hear in each passage:

- Proverbs 19:23
- Luke 12:29–31
- John 1:12; 3:16; 5:24; 6:35, 51; 10:27–28; 11:25–26
- Romans 8:34
- 1 Corinthians 1:9; 10:13
- 2 Corinthians 5:17
- Philippians 4:13, 19
- 2 Peter 3:9

AGE-ALERT TIPS

If you have mostly **older children,** modify the lesson in these ways:

Alert #1: Pass the Bible so children can read the passages aloud.

Alert #2: Add this debriefing question: *Which promise do you find hardest to trust?*

Place cups, open end down, and as close to each other as possible on the cardboard. Then place the second cardboard square on top of the cups, directly over the first square.

To really demonstrate how trust holds us up, ask a lightweight, young child to slowly and carefully lie across the top cardboard square. (For extra safety, have an older child hold the younger child's arms or hands.) The cups should hold up to 80 pounds if the child slowly and carefully distributes his or her weight across the cardboard platform (tell the child not to move).

When the child is laid across the cardboard square, point out how trusting God holds us up—even when it seems impossible! Help the child stand up from the cups. Then discuss these questions as a group:

- **Which of God's promises do you like the most?**
- **Which of God's promises do some people find hard to believe?**
- **Why can we "stand firm" on God's promises and trust him to keep them?**

Say: **Daniel was a man who trusted God to hold him up even when things got tough, and it showed. But it really showed the day Daniel was tossed in a cave full of lions! Let's learn more about what happened in that lions' den and how Daniel learned that God wants us to trust him.**

Bad Days Game

TRUST ME!
Time: 8 minutes or more, as desired
Supplies: none

Ask children to find partners. Jump in if you're needed.

Tell children to look at their partners carefully. Then ask partners to turn back-to-back and ask the person in each pair who's closest to you to change one small thing about his or her appearance. Have partners who aren't making changes close their eyes while their partners are modifying their appearances.

Changes might include taking off glasses, changing a hairstyle, unbuttoning a button, or moving a ring from one finger to another. The partner may also choose to change nothing. Either way, partners will turn at your command and say, "I didn't change a thing. Trust me!" The other partners must then decide what the change was or if *nothing* was changed.

Play several rounds. See how many partners can fool one another by making small changes—or making no changes at all!

Say: **Great job! Not everyone who says "trust me" can be trusted. Today we'll explore whether we can trust God when he asks us to trust him. And we'll discover that answer by looking at the life of someone who did trust God: Daniel.**

Bad Days Bible Story

DANIEL INSTANT THEATER
Time: about 15 minutes
Supplies: Bible

Ask children to spread out in the room. Assign the following roles to your children (a child can play more than one role): King Darius, lions, supervisors, and governors. You'll be the narrator. In a dramatic way, read aloud Daniel 6:1–24 as you encourage your actors to ham it up as you read!

After finishing the reading, applaud the dramatic efforts. As a group, discuss:

- In what ways did Daniel trust God?
- In what ways did King Darius trust God?
- In what ways did the supervisors and governors trust God?
- If Daniel had been eaten by the lions, would God be trustworthy? Why or why not?

Say: I'm glad lions didn't have Daniel for dinner! Daniel trusted and obeyed God even when he thought he was in trouble. Daniel discovered that even when things don't go well, God can be trusted.

God never promised to protect his followers from pain. God promises to love us and promises we'll be with him in heaven, but on earth we get the same broken bones everyone else gets. Listen to what Jesus told his disciples.

Read aloud Matthew 5:10–12 and then ask:

> **AGE-ALERT TIPS**
>
> If you have quite a few **younger children** in your group, try these ideas:
>
> **Alert #1:** Limit the number of roles in the play. Have younger kids be lions who can really roar!
>
> **Alert #2:** Consider reading the story of Daniel in the lions' den from an illustrated children's Bible if you have one. Then have kids provide the sound effects instead of acting out the entire story.

- Why do you think God never promised to keep us safe from lions and the flu and math tests?
- How are we blessed in being able to always trust God to help us?

Say: When tough things happen to me, it helps me to rely on God and to come to him. I know God helps me through hard times. Hard times *do* come along. But even if a lion chases me, I still love and trust God!

CLOSING PRAYER

PUZZLE PIECE PRAYER

Time: about 3 minutes
Supplies: jigsaw puzzle with box

Give each child a puzzle piece. Hide the box lid showing the puzzle art.

Say: **Using your puzzle piece as a clue, tell me in detail what the assembled puzzle looks like.**

Take suggestions before showing the box lid. Point out that it's hard to tell if your puzzle pieces are even *from* the puzzle you showed and that maybe they're from another puzzle altogether!

Say: **Your piece of the puzzle is too small to know what the finished puzzle looks like. You have to trust I'm telling you the truth: your puzzle piece is part of the bigger picture.**

Show the picture of the finished puzzle from the lid. Then say: **Our lives are like puzzle pieces too. We can't see with our own eyes everything God has promised or God has planned for us. We have to trust him— that's just what God wants us to do! Let's thank God for being worthy of our trust as we hold our puzzle pieces and pray together!**

Offer a prayer thanking God for his power to help in our lives as he helped Daniel and for the way we can trust God in all things.

Recover the puzzle pieces after the prayer. Otherwise, whoever loaned you the puzzle will be unhappy on the day he or she assembles the puzzle!

EXTRA-TIME ACTIVITY—OPTION 1

TRUST BUCKET

Time: about 15 minutes
Supplies: newspapers, wastebasket

Give each child a sheet of newspaper to crumple. Place the wastebasket across the room. Allow children to pick a spot from which to toss their paper wads at the basket. Before each shot ask everyone to decide if they trust that the paper wad will end up in the basket. Score a point each time a basket is made.

Play multiple rounds. See who's trustworthy as a sharp shooter and scores highest! Then discuss these questions:

- What made you trust a person's shot?
- What makes you trust someone in other things?
- How trustworthy do you think you are in most things?
- Why is God the best to trust in?

EXTRA-TIME ACTIVITY—OPTION 2

IN GOD WE TRUST

Time: about 5 minutes (or never, depending on your math abilities!)
Supplies: $5 bill for each child—that you'll get back!

Note: This only works with American currency and any dollar denomination works. If you do not have enough five-dollar bills, use one bill and let kids look on together.

Give each child a five-dollar bill (or hold one up and let kids gather to look). Ask children to find the place on the bill (the back, over the Lincoln Memorial) where a phrase appears including the word *God*.

Read the words together and then discuss:

- **In what ways does America show, or not show, it trusts God?**
- **In what ways do you show, or not show, you trust God?**

When you're finished (and if kids all have bills), say: **And now I'm trusting I'll get my money back. Please return my bills!**

EXTRA-TIME ACTIVITY—OPTION 3

INQUIRING MINDS WANT TO KNOW

Time: 5 minutes
Supplies: none

Gather kids in a circle. Ask: **If you were heading into a scary situation, who would you trust to help you? Why?**

Jonah's

Bad Day

The Point: God forgives us.
Scripture Connect: Jonah 1:1–2:10

Supplies for all Session 5 activities options: pencils, prepared poster, 4 hardcover books (that won't be damaged if they fall), 2 bendable wire coat hangers, 2 inflated balloons (plus an extra, just in case!), stopwatch, Bible, a dishpan half filled with water, a plastic bowl or container, silverware (several pieces for each child), salt, 1 bag of salted sunflower seeds, paper

The Basics for Leaders

Many Christians wish they had specific instructions from God. "If he'd just tell me what to do, I'd do it," they say. "I'm willing to follow, but I just don't know which direction to go."

No problem for Jonah. He knew exactly where to go: Nineveh. God even told Jonah what to say when he got there.

Jonah's problem was that he didn't *want* to go, so he ran in the opposite direction, believing that hiding from God would take care of the problem.

Um ... no. Jonah was willfully disobedient—and God didn't let him get away with it.

Jonah's story is familiar to most children who've been in Sunday school. Jonah meets big fish, big fish eats him, Jonah decides if he gets out of fish alive he'll do what God says, fish throws up, and out comes a very stinky Jonah. What gets missed is Jonah's *repentance* ... and God's forgiveness. But without those, Jonah would have ended up fish food.

Today you'll discover an important lesson: *God forgives us.*

OPENING ACTIVITY—OPTION 1

HOWZITGOIN'

Time: about 5 minutes, depending on attendance
Supplies: pencils, prepared poster

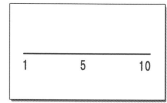

Before kids arrive, draw a line on a poster. Write a 1 on the left end of the line, a 10 on the right, and a 5 in the middle. As kids arrive, ask them to pencil in their initials on the line.

Say: **If this past week was so awful you wish you'd slept through it, place your initials by the 1. If it was a great week you wish you could repeat, put your initials by the 10. Place your initials anywhere on the line that shows how you feel about this past week—except exactly on the 5. Because there's no such thing as a week that's exactly half good and half bad!**

After kids have signed in, give them 30 seconds each to explain why they placed their initials where they did. Be sure to include your own initials and explain your placement on the line. Kids will begin to express themselves more over time, and hearing their stories will help you adapt this lesson to make it relevant to your kids' lives.

OPENING ACTIVITY—OPTION 2

HEAD AND SHOULDERS, KNEES AND TOES

Time: about 10 minutes
Supplies: 4 hardcover books (that won't be damaged if they fall)

Announce that you've decided to bring back an activity that helped their great-grandparents have perfect posture.

Demonstrate with a volunteer how to stand with two books balanced on one's head. Help the volunteer walk without dropping the books. Then form kids into two teams for a relay race.

Ask the first person in each team to walk to a specific spot and then back again without the books falling. If (when!) books fall, children can simply pick them up, balance them, and keep moving forward.

Encourage kids to cheer on one another. When the relay is finished, collect the books and ask children to be seated on the floor to discuss:

- What made it so hard to keep the books from falling?
- After this experience, how would you rate your usual posture?
- You had to keep perfect posture to keep the books in place. What do you do in life absolutely perfectly?

Say: **Most of us don't have perfect posture—or perfect anything else! That's why we need God's forgiveness. And so did Jonah! We'll find out why today.**

Bad Days Game

PERFECT RELAY
Time: 10 minutes or more, as desired
Supplies: 2 bendable wire coat hangers, 2 inflated balloons (plus an extra), stopwatch

Before children arrive, inflate two balloons and tie them. Place the balloons out of sight.

Announce that since the book relay went so well, you'll try another relay (mix up the two teams)—but this time with wire clothes hangers and balloons. Help children bend their hangers for the job of carrying the balloons.

Explain that the goal of the game is for each relay member to carry a balloon on a hanger to the far wall of the room and back. The catch: if the balloon hits the floor, the entire team starts over. Teams must run this relay perfectly. (Fewer than six kids? Work together as a single team!)

Run the first heat of the relay for two minutes (keep track on your watch) and see if any team has completed the course. If so, run it again to see if teams can improve their times.

When the game is over, collect the hangers and balloons. Discuss:

- How did the need to run this relay perfectly affect how fun the game was?
- What in your life do you have to do perfectly? What happens if you don't do it perfectly?

Say: **We know being perfect or doing everything in a perfect way is impossible, isn't it? Let's discover how a guy named Jonah learned that** since we're not perfect, we need a special gift from God—we need God's gift of forgiveness!

Bad Days Bible Story

JONAH SCOOT

Time: about 10 minutes
Supplies: Bible

Ask children to sit close together on the floor, in the center of the room.

Say: **Jonah's story is here in the Bible. As I read, I'll point out different places in the room that represent places Jonah went. When I point to one of those spots, please scoot over to that place.**

With flair, read aloud Jonah 1:1–2:10. Point to the indicated spots when you read these verses:

Chapter 1:

verse 3: Left side of the room (Joppa)

verse 3: Center of room *(getting on ship)*

verse 4: Rock back and forth where seated

verse 5: Right side of the room and keep rocking *(below deck)*

verse 11: Rock back and forth harder

verse 13: Rock back and forth even harder!

verse 14: Scoot to center of room *(going up above deck)*

verse 15: Spin in place *(tossed into sea)*

verse 15: Stop rocking

verse 17: Scoot back to the left of the room *(the fish is swimming)*

Chapter 2:

verse 10: Throw yourself forward as if you were spit out of the fish's belly!

AGE-ALERT TIPS

Alert #1: Have **older kids** read aloud Matthew 6:14–15. Then ask: *How does hearing Jesus's words change how willing you are to forgive others?*

Alert #2: Invite **younger kids** to illustrate the scene when God forgives Jonah—the fish spitting him out.

Finish by saying: **And then, when the Lord told Jonah to go to Nineveh again, that's what Jonah did—so scoot over to the center of the room!** When kids are in place, ask:

- In what ways did God seem angry or demanding?
- In what ways was God forgiving?
- When is a time you knew the right thing to do, but you chose to do the wrong thing? What happened?

Say: **God got Jonah's attention in a yucky way, but he gave Jonah a second chance to make the right choice: the choice to obey God. Jonah still had to suffer the consequences of his bad choice ... three days inside a fish—ugh! But in the end, Jonah was forgiven and got to do the right thing.**

When we disobey, we are punished too. But if we ask God to forgive us, he will. God forgives us and that's good news!

Ask children to select partners and discuss in pairs:

- How hard or easy was it for Jonah to ask God's forgiveness? Why?
- How hard or easy is it for you to ask God to forgive you? Why?

CLOSING PRAYER

BOAT FLOAT PRAYERS

Time: about 7 minutes
Supplies: dishpan half filled with water, plastic bowl or container, silverware (several pieces for each child)

Fill a dishpan half full with water. Float a plastic bowl or container in the pan. Give each child several pieces of silverware that will easily sink when children place all of their silverware in or on the container.

Practice this once so you have the right combination of container and silverware—you don't want the boat to continue floating!

Say: **Jonah thought climbing on a boat heading away from God would keep God from seeing him. Jonah was wrong.**

Our lives are like this little boat. We sail along under our own power and then do something wrong. We sin.

Place a piece of silverware on the "boat."

Say: **Think of things you've done lately that were wrong, that would disappoint God. It might be a lie you told or a mean word you spoke. If there's anything like that in your life, silently tell God about it. For each of those things, place a piece of silverware on this boat. I'll need more than one piece of silverware; I'll bet you do too.**

Continue until the boat sinks. Then reach under the water, empty the silverware, and float the boat again.

Say: **Here's good news: when we tell God what we've done wrong and ask him to forgive us, he does. First John 1:9 says, "If we confess our sins to him, he is faithful and just to forgive us our sins and to cleanse us from all wickedness."**

Let's pray out loud and thank God for his forgiveness. When children are finished, close your prayer time.

Collect the silverware and dishpan and set them aside.

EXTRA-TIME ACTIVITY—OPTION 1

SALT SOLUTION

Time: about 10 minutes
Supplies: a pinch of salt per child, dishpan half filled with water

Place the dishpan in the center of the room. Have children form a circle around it, and place a pinch of salt in each child's hand.

Ask children to think of something they've done that has disappointed God—a sin. Explain that sins are actions and attitudes that don't obey or glorify God. Pause to let children think.

Then ask children to silently ask God to forgive them for what they've done wrong.

One at a time, invite children to toss their pinches of salt into the dishpan. With your hand, gently stir the water as you read aloud Psalm 103:9–14. Invite children to look at the water where the salt dissolved in the water.

Point out that's how God forgives: thoroughly. Once and for all. The punishment of a sin may remain, but the sin itself will be forgiven.

EXTRA-TIME ACTIVITY—OPTION 2

SPITTING CONTEST

Time: about 5 minutes
Supplies: 1 bag of salted sunflower seeds, 1 sheet of paper

Say: **The big fish spit up Jonah, so let's follow his example!** Line children against a wall so they're spitting sunflower seeds in the same direction. Even better: go outside if weather and location permit. You'll give children seeds to spit in two events:

Distance: Just what it sounds like. Who can spit a seed the farthest?

Accuracy: Place a sheet of paper about 10 feet from the spitting line.

See who can come closest to landing a seed on the paper. Have a great time, but remember to clean up!

EXTRA-TIME ACTIVITY—OPTION 3

INQUIRING MINDS WANT TO KNOW

Time: 5 minutes
Supplies: none

Gather kids in a circle. Ask: **God asks us to forgive others the same way he forgives us. What's something you would find very difficult to forgive?**

Mary's

Bad Day

The Point: God keeps his promises.
Scripture Connect: Luke 2:1–7

Supplies for all Session 6 activities options: pencils, prepared poster, paper, 3 Bibles, 2 metal teaspoons per child, index cards, crayons or markers

The Basics for Leaders

Was the day Mary gave birth to Jesus really a "bad day"?

Of course not—it was Jesus's birthday on earth! It marked the arrival of a Savior, news that set angels to singing.

But having a baby is hard work for mothers, and Mary was in a foreign town, far from family and friends.

And when Mary gave birth to God's Son it was where Mary, and the whole world, would least expect God's Son to be born. It was in a stable-cave surrounded by animals!

In this session, you'll help children discover that Jesus's birth in a Bethlehem stable wasn't an accident and not really a bad day at all. God was keeping a promise he'd made years before—and God keeps his promises.

OPENING ACTIVITY—OPTION 1

HOWZITGOIN'

Time: about 5 minutes, depending on attendance
Supplies: pencils, prepared poster

Before kids arrive, draw a line on a poster. Write a 1 on the left end of the line, a 10 on the right, and a 5 in the middle. As kids arrive, ask them to pencil in their initials on the line.

Say: **If this past week was so awful you wish you'd slept through it, place your initials by the 1. If it was a great week you wish you could repeat, put your initials by the 10. Place your initials anywhere on the line that shows how you feel about**

this past week—except exactly on the 5. Because there's no such thing as a week that's exactly half good and half bad!

After kids have signed in, give them 30 seconds each to explain why they placed their initials where they did. Be sure to include your own initials and explain your placement on the line. Kids will begin to express themselves more over time, and hearing their stories will help you adapt this lesson to make it relevant to your kids' lives.

OPENING ACTIVITY—OPTION 2

GUESS WHO'S COMING TO TOWN?
Time: about 15 minutes
Supplies: pencils, paper

Ask children to think of favorite famous people or cartoon characters and then do impersonations. See if your larger group can identify who is being impersonated. Then help children form pairs. (If there's an uneven number of kids, jump in as a partner.)

Say: **Congratulations! A famous person is coming to town! You and your partner are the "advance team" for the visit.**

You'll decide what the famous person—the celebrity—will do, where the celebrity will stay, and who the celebrity will meet. But first you and your partner need to decide which celebrity you'd like to come visit.

So pick a famous sports or movie star, your favorite singer, or even the president. But you and your partner must agree on which celebrity you'd most like to meet. Talk it over—fast. You've got 60 seconds.

After one minute, draw attention back to yourself.

Say: **Your celebrity will be here just one day, so decide where he or she will eat breakfast, lunch, and dinner. What will the person do during the day? Will you need a limo? And where will your celebrity sleep at night?**

You've got four minutes to plan your celebrity's visit. Hey! If you decided on a musician, how about a free concert at your school? If that's what you'd like, put it on the list!

Distribute pencils and paper in case kids want to make notes. Give a two- and one-minute warning and then ask pairs to report to the larger group:

- What celebrity they're bringing to town—and why.
- What that celebrity will do during the day.

Say: **Great work! You took great care of your celebrities! Now with your same partner, decide how you'd care for another famous person if he came to town in person: Jesus.**

Give pairs an additional three minutes to plan Jesus's day in town. If necessary, help with suggestions. Ask pairs to report back their plans.

> **AGE-ALERT TIPS**
> If you have quite a few **younger children**, you may wish to modify this activity in one of these ways:
> **Alert #1:** Pair younger kids with kids a bit older. Encourage older kids to ask younger ones for their ideas often!
> **Alert #2:** If desired, provide crayons, markers, and paper for younger kids to illustrate their plans for the famous person's visit.

Say: **Were Jesus to visit in person, we'd make sure he had the best of the best. He'd get great meals and a comfortable bed. After all, he's the king of the universe!**

God could have given Jesus all that—and more—but God had promises to keep. God said Jesus would be humble and born in Bethlehem. So Jesus's birthday wasn't what people waiting for the Savior expected.

We'll find out more about Jesus's birthday, but first let's find out about yours.

Bad Days Game

YOU WERE SO YOUNG AT THE TIME
Time: 5 minutes or more, as desired
Supplies: none

Ask children to share details of their births if they know the details.

Have children sit on the floor in a circle. Use the following qualifiers (and any you'd like to add) to have children move a specific number of spaces (you decide how many each time) to the left or right in the circle. For example, you might say: "If you were born in a month that begins with the letter *J,* move two spaces to your left."

And you're right: kids will end up sitting on each other!

- If you were born on an even-numbered day …
- If you were born in a hospital …
- If you were born in a town other than this one …
- If you've ever seen a picture of yourself right after you were born …
- If in that picture you look like an alien or a salamander …
- If you were born in a month beginning with the letter M …
- If you were born in a car, an ambulance, or at home …
- If you were born in the first half of your birth month …
- If you think you were the cutest baby ever …

Say: **Great job! Your birthdays were pretty special and not all the same. But there's one special birthday that's unlike any other in huge ways. It's Jesus's birthday, the day he was born to Mary in Bethlehem!**

God kept a lot of promises that day. Let's find out what they were!

Bad Days Bible Story

BABY IN A BARN
Time: about 15 minutes
Supplies: 3 Bibles, 1 metal teaspoon per child, 1 sheet of paper and pencil per group

Give each child a spoon.

Say: **Some famous people throw fits when things aren't perfect. You'll use spoons instead. As I read the story of Jesus's birth in Luke 2:1–7, listen for things that were hard, frustrating, or worrisome for Mary. When you hear something, drop your spoon. I'll stop so you can explain what's wrong.**

Here's where you can expect spoons to drop:

- verse 3: Mary and Joseph were forced to travel.
- verse 5: Mary was about to have a child and was far from home.
- verse 7: No room at the inn.
- verse 7: Jesus was laid in a manger, not a nice crib.

When you've completed reading the passage, gather the spoons.

Say: **Christmas scenes usually show a cozy, clean barn, with everyone gazing down at a wooden manger where, tucked in clean hay, baby Jesus naps peacefully. Not likely.**

The manger was probably a feeding trough carved out of stone, and the stable a cave tucked into a hillside, perhaps even under the inn. It was dark. Smelly. And having a baby can be painful and tiring. Just imagine how tired and uncomfortable Mary must have been. You'd think God could do better for his Son.

AGE-ALERT TIPS

Alert #1: Have **older kids** share their insights through silent dramas, acting out the promise. Or form two groups, and ask groups to find and read the passages themselves.

Alert #2: Invite **younger kids** to draw a picture of the manger scene. Read the passage aloud again and ask children to point out pictures in their drawings that show how God's promises were kept.

Form children into two groups. Give each group a Bible.

Say: **There's a reason Mary had to put up with a tough day giving birth to Jesus. It was so God could keep promises he made hundreds of years before Jesus was born. God shared his promises with people who then wrote them down.**

Ask the first group to find and read Micah 5:2. Ask the second group to find and read Isaiah 42:1–2. Provide help if necessary.

Say: **In your group, find God's promise about Jesus and put it in your own words. You'll share the promise with the other group, so write down what you'll say.**

Allow up to five minutes for groups to read, talk, and rephrase. Float between groups, and if necessary, help children stay on track.

In five minutes (or before if groups finish earlier), ask groups to report. Here's what you can expect kids to discover:

- The ruler of all Israel will be born in Bethlehem (Mic. 5:2).
- The "servant" (Jesus) will be gentle and humble (Isa. 42:1–2).

Say: **God keeps his promises! He saw to it that Jesus was born in Bethlehem, and that Jesus's birth—like the rest of his life on earth— was humble and simple. God always keeps his promises, including his promises to you.** Read aloud Romans 8:38–39. Ask children to restate the promise in their own words, and then help children each find a partner to discuss:

- **How does it feel knowing God will be your friend forever?**

Read aloud 1 John 1:9. Ask children to restate the promise in their own words. Then have partners discuss:

- **If God promises to forgive us, why is it hard to tell God what we've done wrong?**
- **What's the best thing about God's promise to forgive us?**

Say: **God takes great care to keep his promises—to Mary, to the world, and to us. Let's thank him for keeping his promises!**

When children have finished talking, move along to the Spoon Prayer.

CLOSING PRAYER

SPOON PRAYER
Time: about 3 minutes
Supplies: 2 metal teaspoons per child

Give each child two spoons. Hold two spoons yourself.

Say: **Hold one spoon in each hand. Practice clanking them together now.** (allow time) **Good job! Now don't clank your spoons together** unless it's in response to something I say during our prayer. Let's pray.

God, thank you for your promises. You promise to forgive us when we confess, when we tell you we've done something wrong. You're so good to us! We've all done wrong things, things we need to confess to you.

If you've done something wrong you need to tell God about, clank your spoons together. (pause)

We believe you'll keep your promise to forgive us, God.

If you trust God's promise, clank your spoons together. (pause)

Please hear us now, God, as we silently tell you what we've done wrong and ask your forgiveness.

Allow up to 30 seconds of silence.

Thank you, God. Thanks for keeping your promises. Amen.

Let's applaud God with spoon-clank applause! Hit your spoons together quickly and make some noise. Then give some people spoon high fives!

EXTRA-TIME ACTIVITY—OPTION 1

SPOON NOSE

Time: about 5 minutes
Supplies: 1 metal teaspoon per child

It is possible to hang a spoon from the end of your nose. Give it a try! Take the kids outside, if you want, but don't lose the spoons! Once spoons are hanging, add the challenge of walking, speaking, turning around in place—and even jogging!

EXTRA-TIME ACTIVITY—OPTION 2

BIRTHDAY CARD

Time: about 10 minutes
Supplies: index cards, crayons or markers

Give each child an index card and ask them to make colorful miniature birthday cards for Jesus.

EXTRA-TIME ACTIVITY—OPTION 3

INQUIRING MINDS WANT TO KNOW

Time: 5 minutes
Supplies: none

Gather kids in a circle. Ask: **If you could ask God to make any promise, what would you ask him to promise—and why?**

The Disciples'
Bad Day

The Point: Jesus takes care of us.
Scripture Connect: Mark 4:35–41

Supplies for all Session 7 activities options: pencils, prepared poster, assorted household objects (3 per child), 5 pennies per child, Bible, paper, drinking straws, tape

The Basics for Leaders

After a long day teaching, Jesus announced that he wanted to cross the lake. "No problem," said his disciples, piling into a boat.

This "lake" isn't like most lakes you've seen. It's nearly 13 miles long and 7 miles wide, and when storms blow in, high waves appear almost instantly. Fishermen on the Sea of Galilee kept one eye on the weather at all times.

The disciples' boat was too far from shore to turn back when clouds appeared and the wind picked up. Soon, waves crashed over the sides of the boat, and even the fishermen on board knew that "no problem" had just become a huge problem. They were sinking–and fast.

And where was Jesus during the disaster? Asleep in the back.

Jesus's disciples shook him awake. How could he possibly sleep through such danger? Didn't he even care? And that's when the disciples discovered, yet again, two amazing things.

First, Jesus had remarkable power. He could silence the wind. He could calm the waves.

And second, he did *both*–because Jesus took care of his disciples.

You'll help children in your group make the same discovery! Not only does Jesus have the power to help when we're in trouble, he loves us and wants to be with us during those times.

OPENING ACTIVITY—OPTION 1

HOWZITGOIN'

Time: about 5 minutes, depending on attendance
Supplies: pencils, prepared poster

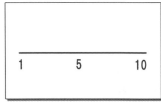

Before kids arrive, draw a line on a poster. Write a 1 on the left end of the line, a 10 on the right, and a 5 in the middle. As kids arrive, ask them to pencil in their initials on the line.

Say: **If this past week was so awful you wish you'd slept through it, place your initials by the 1. If it was a great week you wish you could repeat, put your initials by the 10. Place your initials anywhere on the line that shows how you feel about this past week—except exactly on the 5. Because there's no such thing as a week that's exactly half good and half bad!**

After kids have signed in, give them 30 seconds each to explain why they placed their initials where they did. Be sure to include your own initials and explain your placement on the line. Kids will begin to express themselves more over time, and hearing their stories will help you adapt this lesson to make it relevant to your kids' lives.

OPENING ACTIVITY—OPTION 2

WITH A LITTLE HELP FROM MY FRIENDS

Time: about 10 minutes
Supplies: assorted household objects (3 per child)

Before kids arrive, collect at least three from-around-the-house or from-the-garage objects for each child. Objects can be anything, but the more unusual, the better. Items might include rubber bands, a small trowel or shovel, a clean diaper, a slice of bread, bookmarks, an old ticket stub, pebbles, or *whatever* you can find.

Ask children to form pairs. If you have just a few children, do this activity together as one group. Say: **Wouldn't it be great to be walking down the street, carrying a spare tire, just when a limo pulled over to the curb with a flat? And a famous rock star jumped out saying, "I need a spare tire—now! I'll give the person who's got it free tickets to my show!" One moment you're carrying around a useless tire. The next moment, you're a hero. Here's your chance to be a hero and take care of someone.**

Distribute at least six objects to each pair of kids. Say: **What problems could you solve and what people might you take care of with the objects I'm giving you? You and your partner have three minutes to come up with answers!**

Ask pairs to share what problems they'd solve and who'd they help with their various items. Applaud creativity!

Say: **I'm glad you're so willing to help others! Today we'll explore a situation where someone was willing to help, and he saved lives!**

Bad Days Game

BALANCING ACT

Time: 10 minutes or more, as desired
Supplies: 5 pennies per child

Give children a taste of what the disciples experienced with this fun game! Form kids into pairs, keeping children of a similar size together as much as possible (and pairing younger kids with older kids if needed). Ask pairs to decide who will be the storm and who will be the passenger.

Give each passenger five pennies to stack on the back of his or her left or right hand. Explain that passengers will try to keep the stack balanced and not drop pennies. Ask storms to stand behind their partners and stick their arms directly out.

The storms' goal: to gently bump passengers' shoulders back and forth (never forward) between their arms to cause passengers to drop their stacks of pennies. Storms must also keep their partners from falling!

Say: **Passengers, you'll soon be bumped around like a passenger on a boat during a terrible storm. Keep your balance and don't let your pennies fall overboard.**

Play for half a minute; then have partners switch roles. When each player has been a passenger and a storm, seat kids and collect all of the pennies. Then ask:

- **Which role did you prefer—passenger or storm? Why?**
- **Have you ever felt scared because you were in a situation you couldn't control? What was it?**
- **If you were on a boat and fell overboard in a terrible storm, what do you think would happen?**

Say: **We'll explore a day when Jesus's disciples were passengers during a terrible storm. Jesus was there too, and something truly amazing happened!**

Bad Days **Bible Story**

FACE IT

Time: about 12 minutes
Supplies: Bible

Ask children to sit in a circle. Say: **In a few moments I'll ask you to play a role: a professional fisherman. That means you know the water and boats. You know storms too. You'll play your role by making faces to show how you feel.**

Let's practice. Show me fear. (pause) **No, I mean really show me fear! Look around and see how other people are showing fear.** (pause) **Good! Now show me anxiety ... anger ... joy ... happiness. Perfect! In the historical account I'll share, you'll be the disciples. Some of them were professional fishermen. Ready?**

Read aloud Mark 4:35–41, pausing to encourage faces after verses 35, 36, 37, 38, 41a, and 41b. Then say: **Good job, actors!**

Ask children to scoot around to give each other high fives. Then discuss as a group:

AGE-ALERT TIPS

If you have mostly **older children** (4th, 5th, and 6th graders), modify the lesson in these ways:

Alert #1: If you have a large group, ask capable readers to read aloud.

Alert #2: Let kids stand and use body motions too.

Alert #3: Add this as a last debriefing question: **In what ways has it felt like Jesus didn't take care of you? Why might life sometimes feel that way?**

- How might the disciples tell friends back home about what happened?
- Which was the scariest moment? How much danger were you actually in during that moment?
- Describe a time you think Jesus has helped you.

Say: **You'd think after that example of Jesus's power and his willingness to help the disciples, they'd never have worried about anything again, but that's not true. They were like us: quick to forget, quick to worry, and quick to need a reminder that Jesus takes care of us!**

CLOSING PRAYER

HEAVEN HELP US PRAYER

Time: about 8 minutes
Supplies: 1 sheet of paper and a pencil per child

Say: **I'm glad we can ask Jesus for help. As with the disciples, storms blow into our lives and we feel scared. Jesus wants to help us know that he loves us—no matter what! Let's pray for our families.**

Ask children to write on their papers their home address. Ask young children to draw pictures of their homes. Then have children hold their papers over their heads as you ask God to be with all the people who live under that roof.

Ask children to write the names of family members who don't live with them at their address, or to draw those family members' pictures. Then ask children to hold their papers over their hearts as together you pray for family members to feel God's love during stormy times.

Suggest that children take home their papers as reminders to pray for their families and as reminders that Jesus takes care of them.

EXTRA-TIME ACTIVITY—OPTION 1

BUILD A BOAT

Time: about 8 minutes
Supplies: drinking straws, tape, paper

Place your "building supplies" where children can easily reach them, and issue this challenge: in five minutes or less, each child is to create a "boat" that is steady in a storm.

After children construct their boats, invite them to take extra straws and together blow up a storm, seeing if your wind can blow the boats over!

EXTRA-TIME ACTIVITY—OPTION 2

ROCK THE BOAT

Time: 5 minutes or more, as desired
Supplies: none

Ask children to sit back-to-back on the floor, their backs touching and their heads leaning forward. (Tip: have boys sit with boys, and girls with girls.) Have children cross their arms in front of themselves.

Say: **When I give you the signal, try to rock the boat behind you by leaning back. You can lean back, or suddenly lean forward—your goal is to get the person behind you to lose his or her balance. Ready? Go!** (Caution kids not to crash into each other's backs, but instead push and lean.) Monitor the game.

After two rounds invite children to team up together to take you on in a round. Put up a bit of resistance, then slide sideways onto the floor and let children win. Play several rounds and keep rounds brief.

Say: **Sometimes my boat gets rocked and there's not much I can do about it! The storms are too great and I need help! It's a good thing I can trust Jesus to take care of me!**

EXTRA-TIME ACTIVITY—OPTION 3

INQUIRING MINDS WANT TO KNOW

Time: 5 minutes
Supplies: none

Gather kids in a circle.

Ask: **If you could ask Jesus to fix any one thing that's stormy or troubling in your life right now, what would it be? How would you want Jesus to fix it?**

After children share their answers, remind them they can always trust Jesus to take care of them in any situation.

Lazarus's

Bad Day

The Point: Jesus is powerful.
Scripture Connect: John 11:1–16, 38–44

Supplies for all Session 8 activities options: pencils, prepared poster, straight-backed chairs, Bible, roll of paper towels, facial tissues, paper, tape, various kinds of paper (including newspaper, cardboard, envelope, gift wrap, $1 bill …)

The Basics for Leaders

Two miles.

That's how far Jesus had to walk to reach his friend Lazarus, who was dying in Bethany. But Jesus put off the trip for four days, and rather than come heal Lazarus, Jesus let his friend die.

Picture Lazarus lingering in bed, knowing if Jesus would just come, he'd be healed. Lazarus waited, day after painful day, until at last he could hold on no longer. He died—literally died—as in dead-and-buried died.

We don't know much about Lazarus beyond that he was the brother of Mary and Martha and a friend of Jesus. And that following his death, Lazarus walked out of his tomb once Jesus called him back to life.

Was the day Lazarus died a bad day? It must have felt that way to Lazarus and to his sisters. But four days later, that pain behind them, Lazarus became the reason many Jews came to believe in Jesus.

Lazarus became a living testimony to the truth that Jesus is powerful. And we can do the same!

OPENING ACTIVITY—OPTION 1

HOWZITGOIN'

Time: about 5 minutes, depending on attendance
Supplies: pencils, prepared poster

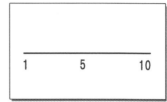

Before kids arrive, draw a line on a poster. Write a 1 on the left end of the line, a 10 on the right, and a 5 in the middle. As kids arrive, ask them to pencil in their initials on the line.

Say: **If this past week was so awful you wish you'd slept through it, place your initials by the 1. If it was a great week you wish you could repeat, put your initials by the 10. Place your initials anywhere on the line that shows how you feel about this past week—except exactly on the 5. Because there's no such thing as a week that's exactly half good and half bad!**

After kids have signed in, give them 30 seconds each to explain why they placed their initials where they did. Be sure to include your own initials and explain your placement on the line. Kids will begin to express themselves more over time, and hearing their stories will help you adapt this lesson to make it relevant to your kids' lives.

OPENING ACTIVITY—OPTION 2

EVERYBODY UP!

Time: about 10 minutes
Supplies: straight-backed chairs

Have children form pairs. Ask the person in each pair whose first name starts with the letter earliest in the alphabet to sit in a chair. (Help younger kids with this.)

Say: **On the count of three, I'd like you to stand up. Ready? One … two … three.** Children will have an easy time rising from the chair. If you have a child who's physically unable to rise from a chair, ask that child to be your helper and give the countdowns.

After they stand, say: **Describe to your partner a time you think it'd be hard to stand up. Maybe it would be on a roller coaster or when there's a bully saying he'll beat you up.**

After several minutes for discussion, say: **You're about to discover another time you can't stand up. It's when your partner has one finger on your forehead.**

Ask the same child in each pair who was just seated to sit in the chair again, this time with arms folded across his or her chest and legs stretched straight out with heels on the floor. The other child in each pair will place a finger firmly against the seated partner's forehead.

Again give a one … two … three countdown. The seated partner won't be able to rise from the seat! Have pairs change places so everyone can take a turn in each role.

Ask partners to discuss:

- **How did it feel to be helpless to rise again?**
- **How is that like or unlike what it's like to die and be buried?**

Say: **You'd think that once you're dead and buried, that's it. You're down and staying down. But for Lazarus death wasn't the end of the story because of Jesus's power. Lazarus rose again! Let's explore what happened.**

Bad Days Game

BOWLINGBASKETSOFTBALL TOSS
Time: 5 minutes or more, as desired
Supplies: none

Ask children to join you sitting in a circle. Tell children you hold an imaginary ball—a basketball. Dribble the ball several times to help kids visualize it.

Say: **When someone tosses the ball to you, you'll change something about it before tossing it along to the next person. For instance, I could make the basketball much larger.** Pretend to stretch the ball until it's huge. **Or I could change the weight.** Shrink the ball, poke three "holes" in it and say: **Now it's a heavy bowling ball!**

Change the ball however you like, but you have to change it somehow before tossing it along, and you can only hold it for seven seconds. Let's see how long we can keep this going!

Toss the imaginary ball to someone in the circle. Encourage creativity. When you've finished, take the ball, shrink it to a marble, and toss it into a pocket. As a group discuss:

- How would this ability make a cool superpower? In what ways could you use it to help and serve others?
- Would you consider someone with a shape-shifting ability powerful? Why or why not?

Say: **Today we'll talk about someone who's really powerful. And who proved it in a way that people have talked about for a long time!**

Bad Days Bible Story

POINT OF VIEW

Time: about 15 minutes
Supplies: Bible, roll of paper towels, facial tissues, pencils

Assign these roles to your children: Lazarus, Jesus, disciples, Martha. If you have just a few children, assign a role to yourself. If necessary, don't assign the Martha role.

Give the child in the role of Lazarus enough paper towels (two or three sheets) to wrap around his or her arm. Give the child in the role of Jesus a facial tissue to hold, because Jesus is sad. Give children in the roles of disciples pencils to hold as knives—they're afraid of being attacked. (Caution kids not to stab anyone with the pencils!)

Hand the child in the role of Martha three paper towels to drape over his or her head as a scarf

After children are ready, say: **I'm going to share an incredible event found in the Bible. As I read, think about how your character experiences the event. What does your character feel? Think? Discover? Use your items to help express yourselves.**

Read aloud John 11:1–16, 38–44. When you've finished, ask children to discuss the following questions from their characters' points of view:

AGE-ALERT TIPS

Alert #1: For **older kids,** add this debriefing question: *If you were Lazarus, how would you go about asking for your money back for your funeral?*
Alert #2: Have **younger kids** play the role of Martha using paper towel scarves. (Do not have younger kids act out roles with sharp pencils.)

- How did your character feel? Why?
- What did your character think of Jesus? Why?
- What did your character learn from this experience? How might this experience change your character's life?

Say: **Can anything be more powerful than raising someone from death? And can anyone be more powerful than Jesus? Lazarus and his sisters learned in an amazing way how powerful Jesus is, and Jesus teaches us about his power in amazing ways too!**

CLOSING PRAYER

BODY PRAYER
Time: about 8 minutes
Supplies: none

Ask children to lie down on the floor, on their backs. Dim the lights.

Say: **I'm going to lead us in prayer by suggesting things we can pray about. With each suggestion, I'll ask you to take a different posture.**

Lying on backs: **Please lie on your backs.** (pause) **The Bible says without Jesus we're dead in our sins. Consider how you'd feel if you didn't have Jesus in your life. Silently tell God.** After a few moments, continue.

Kneeling: **Please kneel.** (pause) **When meeting a king, people sometimes kneel in respect. Tell Jesus why you respect him—why he's powerful and worthy of being called a king.** After a few moments, continue.

Standing: **Now please stand.** (pause) **Jesus said people who love him aren't just servants—they're friends. Thank Jesus for his friendship and love.** After a few moments, continue.

Standing with arms raised: **Now please raise your arms.** (pause) **Jesus is powerful! Praise Jesus for all he is and all he's done!** After a few moments, close with everyone saying "amen."

EXTRA-TIME ACTIVITY—OPTION 1

HEADSTONES
Time: about 10 minutes
Supplies: paper, pencils, tape

Before kids arrive, make a paper headstone for Lazarus. Use the words "Lazarus—friend of Jesus, beloved brother to Mary and Martha."

Give each child a sheet of paper and a pencil. Ask children to think of a famous person who has died and to write or draw a tombstone for that person. Explain that tombstones usually include the person's name and a line or two about what made the person loved or famous. (Invite older kids to help younger kids spell the words for their tombstones.)

After several minutes have kids tape the headstones to the wall. At the same time, tape up the headstone you wrote earlier. Ask children to explain why they picked the person they picked.

When everyone has had a turn to share, point to Lazarus's headstone. Say: **Here's why Lazarus is so special.** Tear down the headstone. **He didn't stay dead! Jesus raised him, and he walked out of his grave. That's something none of the other people you've named here did!**

EXTRA-TIME ACTIVITY—OPTION 2

PAPER FOLD

Time: about 5 minutes
Supplies: various kinds of paper (including newspaper, cardboard, envelope, gift wrap, $1 bill)

Let each child select a piece of paper. Say: **Seems simple enough to fold a piece of paper. I'll bet you're not powerful enough to fold your paper in half eight times. Give it a try**!

After kids attempt to fold their papers in half eight times, ask:

- **Why do you think you couldn't do this simple task?**
- **How powerful do you think you are compared to Jesus? Explain.**

Say: **One way Jesus shows his power is through miracles. I'm sure he could even fold paper eight times! But the way I most like how he shows his power is this:** *he loves us!*

EXTRA-TIME ACTIVITY—OPTION 3

INQUIRING MINDS WANT TO KNOW

Time: 5 minutes
Supplies: none

Gather kids in a circle. Ask: **What could Jesus do that would convince you beyond any doubt he's alive and powerfully working in your world?**

Jesus's

Bad Day

The Point: Jesus loves us.
Scripture Connect: Matthew 27:32–50

Supplies for all Session 9 activities options: pencils, prepared poster, stopwatch, empty soda cans (with pull tabs removed; 1 per pair of kids), 5 pennies per child, Bible, white paper plates, crayons (optional), tape, several wooden cooking spoons, paper

The Basics for Leaders

If there's a way to die more painfully or slowly than crucifixion, the Romans couldn't find it. That's why they reserved crucifixion for criminals—but not most Roman criminals. Crucifixion was considered too painful for Roman citizens, but Jesus wasn't a Roman citizen.

So after being beaten until his back was slashed through to the bone, Jesus was nailed to a cross to die, a public reminder that crossing the Romans was a mistake that brought swift and brutal consequences.

A sad day? Most of Jesus's disciples hid, fearful for their lives. Jesus's mother stood, weeping, watching her son die a criminal's death. It was a day that cut short the life of an innocent man.

A bad day? Not at all—because although he was innocent, Jesus had come to die, to be the sacrifice that let us come to God through him. The Romans weren't murdering Jesus; he was giving his life willingly.

71

For us, that day on the cross was a gift of love that has never been equaled. And it was the first step leading to a day, three days later, that changed everything … forever.

All because Jesus loves us.

OPENING ACTIVITY—OPTION 1

HOWZITGOIN'

Time: about 5 minutes, depending on attendance
Supplies: pencils, prepared poster

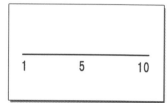

Before kids arrive, draw a line on a poster. Write a 1 on the left end of the line, a 10 on the right, and a 5 in the middle. As kids arrive, ask them to pencil in their initials on the line.

Say: **If this past week was so awful you wish you'd slept through it, place your initials by the 1. If it was a great week you wish you could repeat, put your initials by the 10. Place your initials anywhere on the line that shows how you feel about this past week—except exactly on the 5. Because there's no such thing as a week that's exactly half good and half bad!**

After kids have signed in, give them 30 seconds each to explain why they placed their initials where they did. Be sure to include your own initials and explain your placement on the line. Kids will begin to express themselves more over time, and hearing their stories will help you adapt this lesson to make it relevant to your kids' lives.

OPENING ACTIVITY—OPTION 2

BLINKFEST

Time: about 4 minutes
Supplies: stopwatch

Ask children to pick partners and sit on the floor facing their partners.

Say: **In a few moments I'll ask you to stare at your partner's eyes. We'll see how long we can go without blinking. The average person blinks** about every four seconds—automatically—so keeping your eyes open longer than that will be hard. Ready? Go!

Count off every five seconds. When the last child has blinked, continue.

Say: **Good job! Your eyes will soon be back to normal—the discomfort you might feel will be over in the blink of an eye.**

Today we'll take a look at an event where someone felt real pain that was far worse and lasted far longer. And he experienced that pain not because he had to but because he loves us and wanted to serve us.

Bad Days Game

POINT OF VIEW

Time: 5 minutes or more, as desired
Supplies: empty soda cans (with pull tabs removed; 1 per pair of kids), 5 pennies per child

Say: **When Jesus's friends saw him nailed to a cross, they were very sad. They knew their friend was dead. They didn't really understand that the story wasn't over, that Jesus would rise again. They weren't seeing what happened clearly.** Tell children they'll test how not seeing things clearly can result in poor decisions.

Have each child find a partner, and ask partners to sit on the floor facing each other, at least two feet apart. Give each pair an empty soda can and 10 pennies. Have children set the soda can between them and each child take five pennies. Say: **In a few moments I'll ask you to take turns dropping pennies into your soda can—from at least 12 inches above the cans. It can be done—if you're right on target. But before you begin, close one eye and keep it closed. No cheating! OK, you can begin.**

With one eye closed, depth perception is gone—and so is kids' ability to accurately gauge when to release their pennies. After this round have children again play the game, only this time with both eyes open (and only six inches above the cans, if desired). The pennies should land closer to the opening on the soda cans.

Collect the cans and pennies. Then ask:

- **Why do you think it was easier to be accurate with both eyes open?**

- Tell us a time you thought you saw something clearly, but were wrong?

Say: **Jesus's disciples saw something happen—but they didn't really understand it. They saw Jesus die on a cross. They thought that was the end of Jesus, but it wasn't. Let's dig into what happened!**

Bad Days Bible Story

JESUS PLATES

Time: about 15 minutes
Supplies: Bible, white paper plates, pencils (crayons, if desired), tape

Give each child a white paper plate and a pencil (or crayon).

Say: **We've never seen someone die on a cross—and I'm glad about that. It's such a painful way to die that Romans almost never killed someone that way. They saved that punishment for non-Roman criminals. The torture warned others not to disobey Roman law.**

Jesus was crucified, but we've

AGE-ALERT TIPS

If you have mostly **younger children,** consider reading the story of Jesus's death from an illustrated story Bible. **Young children** may find it hard to illustrate emotions, so having them draw simple crosses on their plates and decorating them with hearts will help them express how they feel.

heard about it so often maybe we don't think about it anymore. It's just a story ... but it happened. As I read aloud an account of what happened to Jesus, listen for words or images that especially move you. Write a word or sketch a picture on your plate to show what happened or how it makes you feel. (Suggestions might include drawing crosses, tears, clouds, or hearts—or writing words such as *sad, painful, sacrifice,* and *love.*)

Read aloud Matthew 27:32–50. Pause often between verses so the story can sink in and so kids can write and draw. Let children work on their art for three to four minutes.

Ask children to show their plates and talk about what they've written or drawn. Then tape the plates to a wall. Depending on how many children's plates you have, create the shape of a cross.

CLOSING PRAYER

FOUND SOUND PRAYER

Time: about 5 minutes
Supplies: several wooden cooking spoons

Hand a wooden spoon to each child or let children share spoons.

Say: **Time to make some muffled music! Think of a song that sums up how you feel about Jesus. Any song—it doesn't have to be one people sing in church. We'll take turns beating out the rhythm on the floor and see if anyone can guess what you're playing.**

Take turns (you're playing too, right?), and when kids have finished say: **We've been praying as we communicated to Jesus what we felt about him. Please close your eyes as I finish for us.**

Briefly thank God for showing his love by sending Jesus. Thank Jesus for giving himself on the cross to die for our sins. Finish by saying "amen."

EXTRA-TIME ACTIVITY—OPTION 1

LOVE LISTS

Time: about 10 minutes
Supplies: 1 sheet of paper and 1 pencil per child

Give each child a sheet of paper and a pencil. Remind everyone that Jesus's death and resurrection demonstrated his great love for us. Then ask children to write "Jesus List" on the top of their papers and list or draw pictures of what Jesus has done—or is doing—that shows how much Jesus loves them. (If you have younger children, pair them with older kids to help them think of ideas to draw on their papers.)

Let children work for several minutes and then report to the larger group what they wrote or drew. As kids report, they can add missed items to their lists.

After sharing, have children turn over their papers and write "My List" at the top. Say: **On this list you'll write or draw what you've done or are doing to show Jesus how much you love him. You'll have three minutes.** (Again, have older kids help younger ones draw their pictures—or simply draw hearts.)

At the end of three minutes, ask children to share what they've drawn with others. Then discuss:

- Which list is most convincing: how Jesus shows his love to us or how we show our love to Jesus?
- What could you do this week that you haven't done before to show Jesus how much you love him?

EXTRA-TIME ACTIVITY—OPTION 2

WHO-LOVES-YOU TOSS

Time: about 5 minutes
Supplies: a penny

Ask kids to form a circle and join them. Explain you'll be tossing a penny to someone in the circle, who will then toss it to someone else. The goal is to keep the penny going as long as possible without having to stop.

And that's the catch: to toss the penny, you have to call out someone or something that loves you. For instance, you might call out "my mom" or "my stepdad" or in a pinch, "my pet guppies."

When you've run out the string of "who loves you" answers, take the penny back and say: **Jesus loves all of us—let's all call out his name because he's shown his love for everyone!**

EXTRA-TIME ACTIVITY—OPTION 3

INQUIRING MINDS WANT TO KNOW

Time: 5 minutes
Supplies: none

Gather kids in a circle. Ask: **We know Jesus loves us. If you could do anything to show your love for Jesus, what would you do, and why?**

The Women's
Bad Day

The Point: Jesus rose from the dead.
Scripture Connect: Luke 24:1–12

Supplies for all Session 10 activities options: pencils, prepared poster, 2 foam cups per child, 1 glass of club soda per 2 children, raisins, metal nuts or marbles, newspapers, Bible, wooden cooking spoons, pillows or other "beatable" objects, 1 clean bedsheet or bath towel, 1 foam ball or ball of crumpled newspaper held by tape, paper, 1 ball of yarn or twine

The Basics for Leaders

Their friend and leader had been killed, and all these women wanted was to be sure he was buried properly.

In Jesus's day, bodies were wrapped in linen cloth along with spices. Then bodies were slid into a tomb. In his case, Jesus's body was placed in a new tomb, one borrowed from a rich follower.

But still, the women came with spices to finish a job that had been done sloppily—hurried along because the Sabbath was quickly approaching. Now was the time to give Jesus's body the respect it deserved.

Except the tomb was open and empty.

Grave robbers? The work of the Romans or Jewish leaders? The people who'd murdered Jesus couldn't even leave his body alone?

But the women found more than just an empty tomb. They found Jesus—alive. Bad day? Yes … but it swiftly got much, much better. What changed it? Jesus rose from the dead!

OPENING ACTIVITY—OPTION 1

HOWZITGOIN'

Time: about 5 minutes, depending on attendance
Supplies: pencils, prepared poster

Before kids arrive, draw a line on a poster. Write a 1 on the left end of the line, a 10 on the right, and a 5 in the middle. As kids arrive, ask them to pencil in their initials on the line.

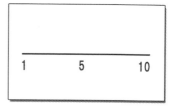

Say: **If this past week was so awful you wish you'd slept through it, place your initials by the 1. If it was a great week you wish you could repeat, put your initials by the 10. Place your initials anywhere on the line that shows how you feel about this past week—except exactly on the 5. Because there's no such thing as a week that's exactly half good and half bad!**

After kids have signed in, give them 30 seconds each to explain why they placed their initials where they did. Be sure to include your own initials and explain your placement on the line. Kids will begin to express themselves more over time, and hearing their stories will help you adapt this lesson to make it relevant to your kids' lives.

OPENING ACTIVITY—OPTION 2

FOAM CUP LAUNCH

Time: about 10 minutes
Supplies: 2 foam cups per child

Foam cups are usually sold in tightly packed tubes or packages, one cup nested in the next. When you give each child two cups, pull the cups apart and gently nest one inside the other *without* pushing them together.

Say: **Here's your challenge: get the top cup that's inside the other you're holding to rise out of it without touching it. And turning over the cups won't work—it leaves the cup lower, not higher!**

Allow kids to try to solve the challenge for several minutes. Then demonstrate the solution: Blow across the lips or edges of the cups. You'll push air under the top cup and lift it from the bottom cup. (Hint: practice this trick before kids arrive!)

Allow children to master the technique (they'll want to show their friends!) and then discuss:

- **What gave the top cup the power to rise?**
- **Christians believe that they'll rise to new life after their bodies die. What will give them power to rise like that?**

Say: **Several women went to the cemetery to honor a dead friend and discovered he'd done some rising too. Let's find out more about that!**

Bad Days Game

DOWN AND OUT

Time: 5 minutes or more, as desired
Supplies: 1 glass of club soda per 2 children, raisins, metal nuts or marbles, newspapers

Ask children to form pairs. (Pair younger kids with older ones for this activity if possible.) Give each pair one glass of soda, one metal nut or marble, and one raisin. Cover a table or floor area with newspapers to avoid spills.

Say: **In a moment, when I give you the signal, drop the nut (or marble) into your glass. But before you do, decide as a pair how many seconds it will take for the nut to float back to the surface. Pick an exact time between 10 seconds and 90 seconds.**

After each pair makes a guess, signal the drop and call out the seconds in 10-second increments to 90 seconds. Look disappointed and suggest that they shake their glasses slightly. The nut will never surface.

Say: **Okay, same thing for the raisin. When will it rise toward the surface? Give me a number of seconds.**

After pairs guess, signal the drop and call out the seconds. The raisins will move up and down in the glass, starting somewhere between 40 seconds and 60 seconds. Declare a winning pair and then ask pairs to discuss:

- **Why did the raisin rise and not the nut?** *(Spoiler note: weight and air bubbles)*
- **How did you do with your guesses? Any surprises?**

Say: **That experiment wasn't too tough to call. But if I asked you to predict which two dead people would sit up first, the logical answer would be neither. But it happened, and that's what we'll explore today!**

Bad Days Bible Story

BEATING AWAY THE BLUES

Time: about 15 minutes
Supplies: Bible, wooden cooking spoons, pillows or other "beatable" objects

Give each child a wooden cooking spoon and a pillow or other object that can be hit with a spoon without consequence. (Hint: if you cannot collect enough spoons and pillows for your group, simply let kids beat their hands on their knees or legs.)

Say: **All of us have heartbeats, and when we grow excited or emotional, our heartbeats grow faster. Your resting heartbeat is probably between 60 and 100 beats per minute. Let's say it's 60 beats and match it with our spoons and "drums"** (or beat with hands on legs).

Lead a one-beat-per-second rhythm and encourage children to get in that groove and stay there, softly tapping their pillows.

Say: **I'll read you a Bible account of something that happened long ago. It's very important because it's the account of Jesus rising from the dead! As you listen, increase the speed of your tapping rhythm when you think the women in our story felt their heartbeats go faster. Slow down when you think their heartbeats slowed down.**

Read aloud Luke 24:1–12. Pause slightly between verses as you lead kids in tapping out the imaginary heartbeats. Then ask children to put down their spoons, find partners, and discuss:

* When do you think the women's hearts beat fastest?
* If you'd been at the tomb, how would you have acted?
* Think about your own heartbeat. What happens to it when you think about Jesus rising from the dead? Why?

Say: **What happened in Jesus's tomb makes a huge difference. It's why we can have hope for life after death. It's why we know Jesus has power. It should fire up our heartbeats!**

CLOSING PRAYER

BLANKET-TOSS PRAYERS

Time: about 10 minutes
Supplies: 1 clean bedsheet or bath towel, 1 foam ball or ball of crumpled newspaper held by tape

Stretch out the bedsheet and have children (and you!) hold it tightly around the edges. Not many children? Use a bath towel. And if you don't have a ball handy, make one by crumpling up newspaper and taping it into a ball shape.

AGE-ALERT TIPS

If you have a lot of **younger children**, try repeating in unison a short, simple prayer such as: "Jesus is alive and we're so glad!" Bounce or toss the ball low until you reach the word *glad*; then toss it high in the air.

Say: **We're going to raise some prayers now. We'll work together to launch and then catch the ball. While the ball is in the air, we'll take turns calling out a word of praise to God for raising Jesus from the dead. I'll go first. We'll launch the ball on the count of three. One … Two … Three!**

Launch the ball and begin by shouting out the word *power* while the ball is in the air. Repeat the ball toss as long as children have words to call out. Keep yourself in the rotation too—you're modeling prayer.

When you're ready to end, ask children to all call out "Amen!" as you launch the ball one last time.

EXTRA-TIME ACTIVITY—OPTION 1

ALL TORN UP

Time: about 10 minutes
Supplies: 2 sheets of paper per child

Give each child a sheet of paper and this challenge: tear the page so there's a roundish-shaped "stone" that rolls in front of an opening in the paper. This is basically tearing the paper so there are two pieces: a circle and the hole the circle makes in the paper. Allow up to three minutes. Ask kids to place their papers down so they can seal up the holes with the stones. Then ask:

- How do you think the women felt when they knew Jesus's body was sealed in a grave?
- What might they have said?

Allow time for children to share. Then ask children to roll away the paper stones, leaving the hole in their papers.

Say: **Jesus didn't stay in his grave. He came back to life!** Ask:

- How do you think the women felt then?
- What might they have said?

After children share, say: **The women's bad day became a very good day because Jesus rose from the dead!**

EXTRA-TIME ACTIVITY—OPTION 2

STRING THEORY
Time: about 5 minutes
Supplies: 1 ball of yarn or twine

Ask children to sit in a circle. Say: **The women who went to Jesus's tomb and found he'd risen from the dead did something right away: they told others! Let's practice telling others something about Jesus.**

Hold an end of the yarn ball and toss the ball to someone across the circle (a "circle" can be two people, by the way!). As you do, share one thing you know about Jesus and can tell to others. Encourage that person to tell something about Jesus and continue the pattern of sharing and tossing.

EXTRA-TIME ACTIVITY—OPTION 3

INQUIRING MINDS WANT TO KNOW
Time: 5 minutes
Supplies: none

Gather kids in a circle. Ask: **If you could tell just one other person about Jesus, and you couldn't tell anyone else, who would you pick? Why?**

Stephen's

Bad Day

The Point: Jesus saves us.
Scripture Connect: Acts 6:8–7:1; 7:51–60

Supplies for all Session 11 activities options: pencils, prepared poster, Bible, 1 fist-size stone, masking tape, newspaper, paper

The Basics for Leaders

This was Stephen's first sermon, and he had a tough audience. The very people who saw to it that Jesus was arrested and killed were in the crowd— and Stephen knew it.

This was the perfect time to try and avoid mentioning things that would arouse the anger of the men who wanted to harm Stephen. But that's not what Stephen did. He told the truth—the *whole* truth—and paid the price for it as a flurry of rocks hurt and killed him.

Bad day? A painful one, certainly, but not a bad one.

Stephen understood that the angry men gnashing their teeth and threatening him weren't his only audience. God was in the audience too, and God was pleased.

Did Jesus save Stephen? Not his body, but Jesus never promised to keep his followers from dying. Jesus saved Stephen's *soul*—something only Jesus could do.

It's true—Jesus saves us!

OPENING ACTIVITY—OPTION 1

HOWZITGOIN'

Time: about 5 minutes, depending on attendance
Supplies: pencils, prepared poster

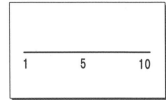

Before kids arrive, draw a line on a poster. Write a 1 on the left end of the line, a 10 on the right, and a 5 in the middle. As kids arrive, ask them to pencil in their initials on the line.

Say: **If this past week was so awful you wish you'd slept through it, place your initials by the 1. If it was a great week you wish you could repeat, put your initials by the 10. Place your initials anywhere on the line that shows how you feel about this past week—except exactly on the 5. Because there's no such thing as a week that's exactly half good and half bad!**

After kids have signed in, give them 30 seconds each to explain why they placed their initials where they did. Be sure to include your own initials and explain your placement on the line. Kids will begin to express themselves more over time, and hearing their stories will help you adapt this lesson to make it relevant to your kids' lives.

OPENING ACTIVITY—OPTION 2

TURN THE KEY

Time: about 10 minutes
Supplies: none

Explain that in a few moments you'll ask one child to leave the room while the rest of the children circle up. (Have a small group? You can be the "circle" alone, if necessary!)

While the "outcast" child is out of earshot, you and the others will decide on one action that opens up your circle and lets the outcast in. It may be touching a nose, blinking twice—anything that the child can do. Don't determine a secret password; it's unlikely the outcast will ever guess that word.

Call the temporarily exiled child back into the room. Say: **You have been shut out of the circle, but there is a way to get back in—if you can guess what it is. You will have help. You can ask five yes and no questions to help you determine what action gets you in the circle.**

If a child guesses the way in, give him or her high fives. If the way in is not determined, choose a new "outcast" and play again. Play several rounds and then have your group discuss:

- **How was this activity like or unlike real life?**
- **What actions get you admitted to the groups you want to join at school?**

Say: **If you want to enter into a friendship with God, there's just one way: through Jesus. A man named Stephen said this, and it created a problem for him. Today we'll explore what happened to Stephen and that even in difficult times, Jesus saves us!**

Bad Days Game

SAVE ME!

Time: 10 minutes or more, as desired
Supplies: none

Say: **There are so many ways you can get in trouble and need help. Let's act some out. I'll call out a situation, and you act out how you'd look if you were in that situation. Ready?**

Here are a dozen situations ... feel free to add your own!

You jumped into the deep end of the pool, and you can't swim.	You walked into the opposite sex's restroom by mistake.
Your bike is about to crash into a wall.	You just found out there's a test, and you're not ready.
You just took a big drink of spoiled milk.	You're late coming home—you decide to sneak into the house.
Your left foot is on fire.	Someone dropped an ice cube down your back.

You fell asleep in class and woke up to find everyone looking at you.

You accidentally glued your thumbs together and have to pull them apart.

You're walking and slip on ice.

You have a heavy box to lift and wish you had some help.

Say: **Great job! You're all qualified to be movie stunt doubles! Get with a partner and find a place to sit as we discuss some important questions!** Discuss:

- **Would you rather be the person giving help ... or getting it? Why?**
- **How do you feel when you have to ask someone for help?**
- **In what ways do you need Jesus's help?**

Say: **We need more than Jesus's help. We need Jesus to save us—**something a man named Stephen discovered. Let's dive into his story!

Bad Days **Bible Story**

TO STONE OR NOT TO STONE
Time: about 15 minutes
Supplies: Bible, 1 fist-size stone

Hold up the stone. Say: **Let's think together,** *What could we do with this stone?*

Take and affirm suggestions. When suggestions slow down, say: **Or we could throw it at someone and hurt him. That would get a reaction!**

Say: **In New Testament times, stones were used a lot of ways. Most of the time it was for building, but if someone blasphemed God or even spoke his name, it was considered**

AGE-ALERT TIPS
This is a long passage for **younger children** to process. If you have mostly **younger children**, modify the lesson in this way:
Alert #1: Paraphrase Acts 6:8–7:1 and 7:57–60. This allows you to soften some of the more brutal parts of this story while still communicating that Jesus didn't spare Stephen's earthly life but brought him into heaven.

disrespectful to God. That person was sometimes punished by having heavy stones thrown at him.

People threatened to punish Jesus with stones because Jesus said he was God's Son. Today we'll explore a time when people punished a Christian named Stephen with stones.

I'll play the part of Stephen. You play the part of the crowd. Let's find out what happens and if Jesus protects and saves Stephen.

You decide if I say anything untrue or if I disrespect God. If so, vote to hit me with a stone. I'll place this stone over here (set it at least five feet from where you'll be as you're reading), **and the first time I say something untrue or disrespectful of God, go stand next to it—but do not throw the stone. Ready?**

Read aloud Acts 6:8–7:1; 7:51–56. Then say: **Okay, it's almost time to vote. But first let's discuss a few questions together.** Discuss the following as a whole group or have kids discuss each with a partner.

- **Has Stephen said anything untrue?**
- **Has Stephen disrespected God?**
- **Do you think it's fair to stone Stephen?**

Ask for a vote. If children want to let Stephen go, have them stand along the wall opposite the stone. If they want to punish and stone Stephen, have them go and stand beside the stone on the floor.

Say: **So we can expect Jesus to save Stephen, right? Let's see!** Read aloud Acts 7:57–60. Ask:

- **What happened in the story?**
- **Why didn't Jesus save Stephen, or did he?**

Listen to and affirm answers. Then say: **Jesus saved Stephen, but not in the way we might have wanted. We think that not being in pain and not dying are the best things possible. But really, being with God in heaven is the best thing. Loving and serving God is the best thing. Following Jesus is the best thing.**

Jesus took great care of Stephen. Jesus just didn't save his earthly life—Jesus saved Stephen's eternal soul. And Jesus can save us too!

CLOSING PRAYER

SAVE ME PRAYER

Time: about 5 minutes
Supplies: none

Ask children to sit in a circle, facing outward so they can't see one another. Say: **In old cartoons when someone is drowning, he raises one index finger when he slips under the water the first time, two fingers the second time, and three fingers the third and last time. We're going to do that too as a prayer.**

I'll mention three things many people need Jesus to save them from. If it's something you need Jesus's help with, raise one, then two, then three fingers. You won't see one another, but God will see you. Please close your eyes.

Pray: **Dear God, we need Jesus to save us. Some of us have done wrong things we need you to forgive through Jesus. If you've done something wrong and need to be forgiven, raise one finger. Silently tell God what you've done.** (pause)

Some of us find it hard to follow you, Jesus. We forget to listen to you. We don't pray, read the Bible, or grow in our friendship with you. If you ever forget to do what Jesus asks you to do, raise two fingers. Tell Jesus about how you need his help being faithful. (pause)

Some of us don't tell others about you, Jesus. If you find it hard to tell friends about Jesus, raise three fingers. Tell Jesus why you find it difficult. (pause)

Please help us, Jesus. Save us from what gets between you and us. Amen.

EXTRA-TIME ACTIVITY—OPTION 1

HORSESHOE SHOES

Time: about 10 minutes
Supplies: masking tape, newspaper

Tape a sheet of newspaper to the floor and position children to stand at least 15 feet away. Ask children to remove their shoes.

Explain that this is a game like horseshoes: a tossed shoe completely on the paper is worth three points, one partially on is worth one point. It's legal to knock another player's shoe off the paper. Play several rounds. Then have children put their shoes back on.

Say: **In some things—like the game of horseshoes—"almost" is close enough to earn points. But in truth telling, being absolutely truthful and not just close to the truth is important. Stephen did that and paid a price. How truthful are you willing to be about Jesus when you have the chance to tell others?**

EXTRA-TIME ACTIVITY—OPTION 2

YOU TOO?

Time: about 5 minutes
Supplies: 1 sheet of paper and 1 pencil for every group

This activity works best with older kids.

Ask children to form groups of two or three. Give each group a sheet of paper and a pencil. If you're playing with young children, be sure to pair them with older kids who can write down answers!

Say: **You're about to play a game called You Too? In two minutes or less, I want you to discover 10 things you have in common. And not easy stuff like "We both have ears" or "We both think you're handsome/beautiful." Find unusual things like "We both speak French" or "We both have 17 letters in our middle names." Write down what you have in common as you go. Ready? Start now!**

At the end of two minutes, ask groups to share some of their You Too? discoveries. After they're finished, say: **Here's another thing you have in common: Jesus wants to save you both. That's something everyone can have in common!**

EXTRA-TIME ACTIVITY—OPTION 3

INQUIRING MINDS WANT TO KNOW

Time: 5 minutes
Supplies: none

Gather kids in a circle. Ask: **If being saved by Jesus is such a smart thing, why don't all people want to have that happen?**

Saul's

Bad Day

The Point: God can use us all.
Scripture Connect: Acts 9:1–8, 19b–22

Supplies for all Session 12 activities options: pencils, prepared poster, paper, Bible, tape, newspaper, thick black markers

The Basics for Leaders

Saul is heading to town to track down and arrest people who believe in Jesus. He's got his posse, his orders from the high priest, his firm belief he's doing the right thing. After all, Christians are claiming that the Messiah has already come, and Saul just doesn't buy it.

Until that Messiah shows up—in a light so bright it knocks Saul to the ground.

Saul hears Jesus's voice, and in one heart-wrenching moment his life is changed. Not only has he been wrong about the Messiah, he's been wrong about hunting Christians. The thing he thought was right was totally wrong.

Plus, dusting himself off, Saul realizes he's blind.

Tough day, but one that set the stage for a wonderful day later in the week. That's when Jesus sent a believer to visit Saul, to help Saul see again and so Saul could be filled with the Holy Spirit.

Saul became a Christ follower, a missionary, a maverick who pushed to carry the message of Jesus to non-Jews. The man who once was an enemy of Jesus became a passionate, focused follower—and a great example of the truth you'll explore today: God can use us all!

OPENING ACTIVITY—OPTION 1

HOWZITGOIN'

Time: about 5 minutes, depending on attendance
Supplies: pencils, prepared poster

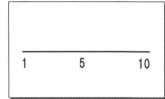

Before kids arrive, draw a line on a poster. Write a 1 on the left end of the line, a 10 on the right, and a 5 in the middle. As kids arrive, ask them to pencil in their initials on the line.

Say: **If this past week was so awful you wish you'd slept through it, place your initials by the 1. If it was a great week you wish you could repeat, put your initials by the 10. Place your initials anywhere on the line that shows how you feel about this past week—except exactly on the 5. Because there's no such thing as a week that's exactly half good and half bad!**

After kids have signed in, give them 30 seconds each to explain why they placed their initials where they did. Be sure to include your own initials and explain your placement on the line. Kids will begin to express themselves more over time, and hearing their stories will help you adapt this lesson to make it relevant to your kids' lives.

OPENING ACTIVITY—OPTION 2

ONE OF A KIND

Time: about 10 minutes
Supplies: 1 sheet of paper and 1 pencil per 2 children

Ask children to form pairs. (If you have young children, consider pairing them with older kids for this activity.) Distribute a sheet of paper and pencil to each pair.

Explain: **I'll give you a category, and I want you to think of five things that fit in it. Write down or draw your answers. If you have something on your list no other pair has, you get a point for that answer. If any other pair has that item on its list, you don't get a point. Your goal: be creative and score some points!**

If you have just a few children, ask for only three items per category, and let each child work on his or her own. It's important you have at least three teams for scoring purposes. Jump in as a team, if necessary.

Here are categories to get you started—feel free to add your own!

- Favorite fast food
- Vegetables
- Pets at the pet store
- Ways to save money
- Brands of soda pop

- Makes of cars
- Sports in the Olympics
- Ways to encourage others
- Holidays
- Zoo animals

Total up the points and then declare everyone a winner. Say: **None of us came up with exactly the same list for each category. We're all different, but we all came up with good answers that helped our teams. That's how it is in life: we're different, but God uses all of us!**

Bad Days Game

SNACK INVASION

Time: 10 minutes
Supplies: none

Before this activity, it may be a good idea to ask permission or clue in the adult group before having kids go on their snack invasion. Tell adults not to act as if they had prior warning of this unusual—and fun—invasion!

Gather kids and remind them that somewhere in the building are a bunch of adults meeting and where there are adults sitting around, there are ... snacks! Together you're going to find out what those snacks are, where they are, and retrieve a sample.

AGE-ALERT TIPS

If you have mostly **older children** (4th, 5th, and 6th graders), modify the lesson in this way: don't let the adults know you're invading—go for broke!

For this mission you'll need volunteers to fill the following roles and make your snack invasion successful. If you have a lot of children, assign more than one child to each role. If you have very few children, assign one child per role and take one yourself, if necessary.

- **Advance Scout:** who will crawl across the floor to avoid being seen and will retrieves a snack *sample* (not all of them, just a sample).
- **Distracter:** who will provide a distraction if the Advance Scout is spotted. This person will walk up to the adult group and draw attention away from the Scout by saying, "I think my belly button is broken."
- **Cover Crew:** who will stay just out of sight, saying things like, "My favorite Bible verse is …" and "Let's look that verse up." This crew makes the adults think your session is still under way.

Say: **To pull this off and get a snack sample, we've got to work together. Everyone has a part to play. Ready?**

Do a bit of quick planning and launch your snack invasion. (If you want to ensure success, tip off the adult small-group leader you'll be coming.)

When children have their samples and are all back in their designated area, discuss:

- **Why was it important we all did our part?**
- **What's another place in life where it's important that we all cooperate and work together?**
- **God can use all of us, but do you think he does? Are there people he can't use? Why?**

Say: **Today we'll explore the story of how God used someone who you'd never thought could be used by God, someone who was actually an enemy of Jesus and the church!**

Bad Days Bible Story

SIGNS, SIGNS, EVERYWHERE A SIGN

Time: about 15 minutes
Supplies: Bible, 1 sheet of paper per child, 1 pencil per child, tape

Before kids arrive, write the words *fair* and *unfair* on two sheets of paper, one word per paper. Tape the papers to opposite sides of the room.

Gather kids in the center of the room and point out the signs. Then say: **Think about the meanest kid you know in school—someone who's a bully.**

This kid is mean to other kids, says hurtful things, maybe even cheats at games or tells lies about others.

Now imagine that the principal gives the bully the very best job in school!

By the way: what is the best job in the school? Raising the flag? Cleaning the restrooms? What do you think?

AGE-ALERT TIPS

If you have **younger children** who may not be able to read well, point out the signs you've taped to the wall and be sure to read them aloud often so everyone knows which choice they will be hopping to throughout this activity.

Allow children to respond and then say: **Yeah, that's it! That's the job! Does it seem fair that a bully gets that great job? Pick one of the signs as your answer and hop over there.**

After kids hop to their choice of signs, encourage them to share their thoughts and explain their reasons for answering as they did.

Then say: **It seems wrong for a bully to have the chance to be the biggest help, doesn't it?**

Today we'll meet a guy who lived in Jesus's time who was meaner than the meanest bully! This guy hated God's people and spent his time chasing, hurting, arresting, and even killing those who loved and followed Jesus! And yet God chose to use him in an amazing way!

Let's read what the Bible says about this guy and how he met Jesus one day. As we read, you'll have more chances to make choices, so hop back to the center of the room.

Read aloud Acts 9:1–2. Briefly discuss what Saul was doing to be mean and hateful to God's people. Then ask: **Was Saul treating God's people fairly or unfairly? You choose. Hop to the sign that shows your answer!**

Ask kids to briefly explain their answers. Then say: **Seems to me that Saul treated Jesus's followers and God's people with unfair hatred. Everyone back to the center of the room.**

Now listen to what happened next—and be ready to make another choice!

Read aloud Acts 9:3–8.

Then say: **Do you think it was fair or unfair of Saul to treat Jesus so badly? You choose. Hop to the sign that shows your answer.**

When kids have chosen, ask children to briefly explain their decision and then to return to the center of the room.

Say: **Saul treated Jesus and his followers in unfair, wicked ways—and yet Jesus came to Saul and spoke to him.**

Read aloud Acts 9:19b–22 and then say: **God told Saul to change his heart and life, and Saul began to serve and obey God. Do you think it was fair or unfair for God to give Saul a second chance and give Saul an important job to do? You choose and hop to the sign that shows your answer.**

Ask children to briefly explain their answers again. Then say: **Saul was a mean, hateful guy—a bully—until Jesus appeared to him and God chose Saul to serve him. Fair or unfair, God used Saul in amazing ways. And if God can use a bully like Saul in great ways, just think how God can use you!**

CLOSING PRAYER

CROSS-EYED PRAYER

Time: about 5 minutes
Supplies: 2 sheets of paper and a section of newspaper for each child, thick black markers

Before kids arrive, draw a cross on a sheet of paper. (Be sure you use very thick black markers for this activity!) Make the cross about four inches high and three inches across. You'll use this sample to show kids during the activity so they know approximately how large to draw their own crosses.

Give each child two sheets of paper and a section of newspaper. The newspaper is to place on the floor as a work surface—you don't want a marker to stain the floor!

Ask children to place one sheet of paper on the newspaper and place the extra sheet of paper on their laps. Then have kids use markers to each draw a cross on the sheet of paper sitting on the newspaper. Encourage children to make the vertical and horizontal lines of the cross thick and solid.

Say: **In a few moments I'll ask you to hold your cross picture about a foot in front of your face and stare at it. Then, as quickly as you can, you'll switch that sheet of paper with the blank one on your lap. You'll hold the blank sheet of paper the same distance from your nose. Let's practice once.**

Once children have practiced, say: **Now hold your cross about a foot in front of your face and stare at it for 30 seconds. I'll tell you when to switch papers.**

When 30 seconds have passed, tell children to quickly make the switch with their clean sheets of paper and stare at them instead. They should continue to see the cross as an afterimage. Ask children what they see.

Have children put down their papers. Say: **Keeping our eyes on the cross—on Jesus—is what Saul did. He met Jesus in a life-changing encounter, and from that day forward he never took his eyes off Jesus, never forgot what happened on the cross.**

Let's ask God to keep us mindful of what he's done for us, and ask him to use us in any way he wants. Ask your children to join you in prayer.

Pray: **God, help us keep our focus on Jesus and to always remember that he can use each of us. We want to be used by you, Jesus. Show us how. Amen.**

EXTRA-TIME ACTIVITY—OPTION 1

INSTANT TALENT SHOW

Time: about 10 minutes
Supplies: none

Yep, God can use us all … starting now.

Encourage children to give God their talents by holding an impromptu talent show where children can juggle, dance, sing, tell jokes, impersonate people (maybe you?), or whatever else they enjoy doing.

Encourage, but don't force, everyone to participate. Then discuss:

- **How might God use your talent—or another one—in the next week?**
- **Why is letting God use your abilities a good idea?**

EXTRA-TIME ACTIVITY—OPTION 2

NEWSPAPER HUDDLE

Time: about 5 minutes
Supplies: 1 sheet of newspaper

Place a sheet of newspaper on the floor.

Say: **Who can God use? All of us! Let's celebrate how we all fit in God's plans, by all standing on this sheet of paper. How can we stand so we all fit?**

After kids sort out a way to fit, fold the sheet in half and invite them to do the same thing again. (Hint: one easy way to put lots of people on a sheet is for them to stand on one foot, lean back, and balance one another by holding on.)

After you've gotten the paper as small as possible and still fit, ask children to sit. Say: **We're all different and so are our feet! Yet there was a place for all of us on the paper.** Ask:

- **How is that like fitting into our church and church family?**
- **Where do you fit in serving Jesus?**

EXTRA-TIME ACTIVITY—OPTION 3

INQUIRING MINDS WANT TO KNOW

Time: 5 minutes
Supplies: none

Gather kids in a circle. Ask: **If you could pick how God would use you, what would you ask him to help you do and help you become?**

A Jailer's

Bad Day

The Point: God desires action, not just words.
Scripture Connect: Acts 16:25–33

Supplies for all Session 13 activities options: pencils, prepared poster, $1 bill per 2 children (bills will be returned!), Bible, 1 pair of adult-size tube socks for each child (clean, various colors, will be returned)

The Basics for Leaders

No one knows if the jailer who locked Paul and Silas in stocks enjoyed his job, but we do know he took it seriously. Good thing too, because he worked for the Romans, and they took prisoners very seriously.

So seriously, in fact, that Roman law held that jailers shown to be careless and let prisoners escape, were killed.

Imagine then how the Philippian jailer felt when he awoke to an earthquake that sent walls tumbling and broke open his prisoners' stocks.

A bad day for the jailer? A horrible day!

He drew a sword, prepared to take his own life before the Romans could reach him. Drawing back the blade, he heard Paul's announcement from the rubble that no prisoner had escaped. The prisoners had time to run away, but they hadn't done so.

What had been the jailer's worst (and almost last) day of his life took a sudden turn. He not only kept his job, but the actions of Paul and Silas convinced him that the Jesus they followed was worth a careful look.

It wasn't Paul and Silas's preaching that brought the jailer to Jesus; it was their actions … and actions speak louder than words.

OPENING ACTIVITY—OPTION 1

HOWZITGOIN'

Time: about 5 minutes, depending on attendance
Supplies: pencils, prepared poster

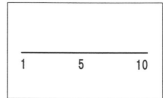

Before kids arrive, draw a line on a poster.
Write a 1 on the left end of the line, a 10
on the right, and a 5 in the middle. As kids
arrive, ask them to pencil in their initials on
the line.

Say: **If this past week was so awful you wish you'd slept through it,
place your initials by the 1. If it was a great week you wish you could
repeat, put your initials by the 10. Place your initials anywhere on the
line that shows how you feel about this past week—except exactly
on the 5. Because there's no such thing as a week that's exactly half
good and half bad!**

After kids have signed in, give them 30 seconds each to explain why
they placed their initials where they did. Be sure to include your own
initials and explain your placement on the line. Kids will begin to express
themselves more over time, and hearing their stories will help you adapt
this lesson to make it relevant to your kids' lives.

OPENING ACTIVITY—OPTION 2

MOVE FAST!

Time: about 10 minutes
Supplies: $1 bill per 2 children (you'll get the bills back!)

Ask children to pick partners. Give the partner who has the longest hair in
each pair a one-dollar bill—and mention you'll want it back!

Explain that the person with the bill will hold it vertically from one end.
The other person in each pair will hold his or her thumb and index finger
four inches apart, several inches below the bill, and will attempt to catch
the dollar bill when it's dropped. It takes quick, catlike reflexes—or a bit of
luck!

After several tries to catch the bill, reverse roles so each partner can both drop and catch (maybe!) the bill.

Collect the bills and then discuss:

- **Which role did you prefer: dropper or catcher?**
- **What helped you catch the bill, if you did?**
- **If you could stretch time and have all of it you wanted for any activity that's usually rushed, what activity would you pick? Why?**

Say: **Sometimes it helps accomplish a goal if we move fast and sometimes if we move more slowly. Today we'll consider a situation where there was time to do something you'd expect people to do but nobody moved. Curious? Let's find out more!**

Bad Days Game

HUMAN LOCKER ROOM

Time: 8 minutes or more, as desired
Supplies: none

Say: **Anybody can build a human pyramid—you just pile people on top of one another. We're going to do something far more challenging: we'll build other kinds of structures using just our bodies!**

If you have very few children in your group, that's fine, just modify your list. Most of the suggestions provided work well for two or more people. Give children just 30 seconds to "build" each structure you mention. Be encouraging and applaud creativity. Suggest that children work together to build some of the following using their bodies. Be sure to build a jail first.

- a jail
- a tepee
- the Leaning Tower of Pisa
- the Eiffel Tower
- a shower stall
- the Statue of Liberty
- a locker room

When kids have finished building their structures, applaud their efforts. Then ask them to discuss these questions:

- **If you could move your room to any famous building and live there, what building would it be, and why?**
- **Of the buildings we built, which do you think would hold up best in an earthquake? Why?**

Say: **Our Bible story involves a building we constructed: a jail. It didn't hold up well in an earthquake; the walls fell. But that let the apostle Paul and his friend, Silas, make a big impression on a jailer. Let's see how!**

Bad Days Bible Story

SOCK PUPPET THEATER

Time: about 15 minutes
Supplies: Bible, 1 pair of adult-size tube socks for each child (clean, various colors, will be returned)

Even if you have just a few children at your meeting, you can still assign every part in this play. Each child can play two parts by putting a sock on each hand!

Ask children to sit in a circle. Cast these parts: Paul, Silas, prisoners, jailer, and the jailer's family. Make extra kids prisoners or the jailer's family.

Say: **Actions speak louder than words, and God desires us to have active faith. Let's test that by doing this puppet show with no words other than the narration. Your puppet can't talk, but it can move. Communicate the actions I describe by using movement. For a stage we'll use our imaginations. Ready?**

Read aloud Acts 16:25–33. Pause after each verse and whenever there's movement described. When finished, encourage the actors to take a bow. Collect the socks and then ask:

- **How did Paul and Silas's actions affect the other prisoners?**
- **Why did Paul and Silas's actions have such an impact on the jailer?**

- How do your actions affect people around you? How would you like your actions to affect others?
- How can both your words and actions tell others about Jesus as Paul and Silas's did?

Say: Paul could have told the jailer about how Jesus could save him, and, Paul later did just that. But when Paul showed the jailer what it meant to be saved, that made a huge impact. Paul's actions spoke loudly and then the jailer could hear Paul's words. God desires our faith to be active, not just expressed by words alone. Actions do speak louder than words!

CLOSING PRAYER

EARTHQUAKE PRAYER

Time: about 5 minutes
Supplies: none

Say: Paul and Silas were locked in a jail, and God set them free, through an earthquake. Usually earthquakes are thought of as natural disasters. Nothing good happens in them, no good comes out of them. But God works through nature in powerful ways. Let's thank God for working through his creation to do his will. Even in the middle of an earthquake, hurricane, or tornado, God can bring about good things.

Think of a natural disaster that scares you, and hold your hands in a shape that reminds you of it. For instance, if you're scared of hurricanes, you might make a giant O—the shape of a hurricane. Ready? Then close your eyes, please, and let's pray.

Pray: God, you see our hands. You see our hearts. You know how much damage an earthquake can cause, but you still used one to help Paul and Silas and the jailer who came to you.

When scary things happen in nature or troubles happen in our lives, help us put our faith into action by trusting your power to help and love us. In Jesus's name, amen.

EXTRA-TIME ACTIVITY—OPTION 1

TWO LIES AND A TRUTH

Time: about 10 minutes
Supplies: none

Tell children to think of three facts about their lives that others may not know, such as a middle name or a secret talent or someone famous they may have met. The catch: two facts will be true, and the third will be a lie.

Ask children to form pairs and tell their partners the three facts. The goal is for each child to correctly identify which of the "facts" are true and which one is false.

Ask partners to report how they did and what they learned about each other.

Say: **The jailer who heard Paul's voice after the earthquake in Philippi thought he was hearing a lie.** *The prisoners hadn't escaped? How could that be?* **But he discovered that Paul was telling the truth!**

And not only did Paul tell the truth but he acted on it too. Paul knew that God wants us to put our faith into action and not just words. It's good to remember that actions often speak louder than words!

EXTRA-TIME ACTIVITY—OPTION 2

SHOW ME, DON'T TELL ME

Time: about 5 minutes
Supplies: none

Actions better speak louder than words, because there aren't any words used in this activity!

Ask children to communicate messages through actions only—no writing or speaking. If desired, form two groups and take turns acting out the following and having the other team guess what's being communicated.

You can add your own messages, but here are six to get you started:

- Fire! Come with me to safety!
- Don't drink the water.

- I've got ants in my pants!
- I'm riding a camel.
- I've got 10 million dollars and it's all in quarters.
- I want a glass of iced tea.

INQUIRING MINDS WANT TO KNOW

Time: 5 minutes
Supplies: none

Gather kids in a circle. Ask: **What action speaks loudest to you if someone is saying, "I want to be your friend"? What actions speak loudest in telling your friend about Jesus?**

WE SERVE A BIG GOD.
Show kids how big!

Kids will discover, think about, talk about, pray about, and apply what they learn.

Each book in this series includes 13 easy-to-lead, undated sessions to help elementary kids discover the faith-building, life-changing truths tucked into God's Word. So be sure to get them all! 13 weeks of fun for $12.99.

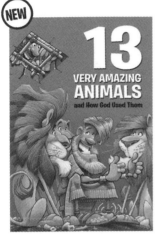

13 VERY AMAZING ANIMALS AND HOW GOD USED THEM
ISBN 978-1-4347-1254-7

13 VERY AWESOME PROMISES AND HOW GOD ALWAYS KEEPS THEM
ISBN 978-0-7847-3359-2

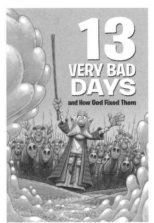

13 VERY BAD DAYS AND HOW GOD FIXED THEM
ISBN 978-0-7847-2122-3

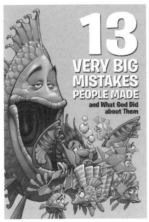

13 VERY BIG MISTAKES PEOPLE MADE AND WHAT GOD DID ABOUT THEM
ISBN 978-0-8307-7258-2

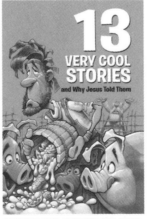

13 VERY COOL STORIES AND WHY JESUS TOLD THEM
ISBN 978-0-7847-2123-0

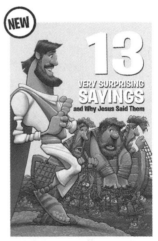

13 VERY SURPRISING SAYINGS AND WHY JESUS SAID THEM
ISBN 978-1-4347-1255-4

Available from your Christian retailer or David C Cook

DAVID C COOK

transforming lives together